Perfectly Imperfect

Unleashing Your Purpose After Pain

Shaneé McCambry

Other Books by Shaneé McCambry

Perfectly Imperfect: Unleashing Your Purpose Guided Journal

You can check for updates on new books and events at:

https://www.ThePerfectlyImperfectBook.com

Dedication

This book is dedicated to my Mom, Pamela Binion; my Granny, Ruth Binion; and my late Aunt, Ann Laura Stinson. I cannot thank you enough for showing me the power of strength, resilience, and hard work in the face of doubt and tough times. You did the best with what you had and what you knew. You have taught me, in your own unique ways, to make sure I bloom where I'm planted, even in the darkness.

To my daughters, Raegan and Rylee, may you always remember you are a light in this world, and never let anyone steal that God-given light and joy. Don't ever let anyone tell you that you can't do something. Accept any challenges that may come your way with a smile, positive energy, and face that challenge with everything that makes you YOU.

May the Lord continue to watch over, guide, protect, and keep you both safe. I am so very proud of you and blessed that God chose me to be your mommy. I love you girls!

Last but not least, to any girls, young women, or women, who have ever felt dimmed by doubt, felt their voice silenced by fear, or have set their dreams or desires to the side due to feeling unworthy, inadequate, or unvalued, this book is dedicated to you, too.

May it be a reminder that we are not alone, especially in those moments when we feel are the darkest and have hit rock bottom. I pray this book helps you on your journey of releasing your burdens, finding your voice, and turning your traumas into triumph.

You are not alone. I see you. I believe in you.

Contents

Chapter One

Second Time's the Charm, Right?

It took me a long time to step into my own power. Even when writing this book, I experienced doubt. What if telling the truth hurt somebody? Surely, some people would be upset to hear that their actions affected me negatively. Wouldn't it be better to just keep quiet?

The answer was "no."

I have seen the power of speaking the truth, in my personal life and in the world at large. In my lifetime, I have seen things get better for women and for so many groups of people because enough of us stood up and told the truth.

In my personal life, I have felt what it is to step into my own power, after decades of feeling inadequate and afraid.

Some of you may know me as Shaneé McCambry. Chief Operating Officer of Inc. 5000 company Novae, wife of Reco McCambry, Founder and CEO of Novae, award winning entrepreneur and consultant. My titles only matter because today, I am the sort of person I never would have thought I could be years ago.

There was a time when I felt like a complete and utter failure. So much so that I tried to end my life. Twice.

How could I feel this way? Even back then, on paper my life was pretty great. Sure, I had my failures. I dropped out of college at one point. But I was also a star cheerleader and a Homecoming Queen with *three* parents who were trying their best to be supportive.

So how could I feel so bad about myself?

Many of us struggle with these secrets, seemingly irrational senses of inadequacy. Many of us hesitate to take the plunge because we don't believe that we can rise to the occasion, hesitate to promote ourselves because we don't think we deserve it or because we feel it would be wrong to act like we're somebody. And don't get me started on self-sabotage.

Too many of us are held back by these feelings. Held back from success and held back from that bone-deep full-body feeling of wellness we deserve.

Psychology, and my own personal experience, have some things to say about why this is. Countless authors have written about the ways in which women are often trained not to give themselves credit, to be afraid of self-promotion, to feel inadequate unless they are serving somebody else. And how this often, paradoxically, impairs our ability to really serve the greater good.

But let's make this concrete. In my experience, glittering generalities are not as helpful as a true story. So I am going to share my story. And I hope that, after reading it, a whole lot of you might feel less alone.

In this book, I am going to share as much of myself as I can. I am going to share the parts I've been afraid to talk about because they're not glamorous, because they're not "successful," and because, to be honest, I was afraid of being judged or "punished" if I spoke the truth.

I'm not afraid anymore. And I hope that in this book, in the work that I encourage you to undertake in your own life, you will find a sort of freedom too.

In addition to the story of my first few decades of life, this book contains questions and exercises to help you explore your own experiences. These are best done with a friend or a support group, if you can get one.

This book is designed to help you to support yourself if you must, but we are most powerful when we support each other.

Now, prepare yourself for some potentially disturbing scenes to come. We will discuss attempted suicides, child molestation, and more as we dive into the pains and fears that hold so many of us back—and bring them out into the light, so that we can see our strength for what it is, instead of seeing it as weakness.

***

The second time I tried to kill myself, I was determined not to make a mess. I was already imposing on my brother enough as it was. While my friends were all starting their careers, Monta was letting me crash at his place because of the arguments happening at my parents' house. I was a college dropout who couldn't put $5 in my gas tank.

For years, I'd had the creeping sense that I was a burden to my family. It was hard to pinpoint where this feeling came from, since on the face of it they seemed happy to support me materially. Monta was happy to have me stay with him; my mom and stepdad were happy to pay for me to live off-campus at my college. So why did I feel like a burden when everyone kept telling me I wasn't one?

I took the pills and then walked out to my car. I didn't want Monta to find me dead in his house and have to think about that every time he came home. This way my family could just get rid of the car and never have to think about it again. Out of sight, out of mind had always been the policy around here. They could forget about me just like they forgot about all the other things that hurt to think about.

I didn't leave a note because that would give them something to think about. It might make it seem like there was something someone could have done, when really this was my problem. Everybody else did what they were supposed to do. I was the only one who couldn't seem to.

So I walked out to my 20-year-old Honda Accord and got in the driver's seat and waited. Waited to feel sleepy. Waited to pass out. Waited to die.

Nothing happened.

I drummed my fingers on the steering wheel in frustration. As the minutes ticked by, as the minutes became an hour, the tapping turned into slamming my fists on the steering wheel in frustration. Nothing was happening.

Again.

Nothing had happened the first time I tried to die, either.

There was sunlight filtering in through the windshield. The afternoon was quiet around me. But this wasn't an "I'm grateful to be alive" moment. I was *mad.*

Why are you keeping me here? What am I supposed to do?

I slammed my hands on the steering wheel one last time and took a deep breath. I didn't understand *why* God would make me stay here. Deep down, I had the sense that nobody really wanted me around.

And *that* was the problem.

I'd spent my life being told that my feelings were an inconvenience. *I* was fine—as long as I did the things I was supposed to do, played nice, went to college, and all that. My family would even catch me with a roof over my head when I fell.

But emotionally speaking, that was another matter.

I grew up feeling crazy for being so emotional. I was surrounded by hard-working individuals who tried their best to love and support me. I knew many people would have felt lucky to have that. My family wasn't rich by any means. But we were compared to my friends whose parents didn't have a penny to put toward their education, whose siblings didn't have a home where they could stay, who didn't have food on the table or running water consistently, we were lucky.

So why was I so unhappy? Why did I feel like everybody would be better off if I weren't there?

I realize now that I felt that my emotions were a problem. That the "me" who "wasn't a burden" wasn't the real me. I was welcome and supported as long as I played my role properly, but there was so much that had happened to me that we never talked about. So much I was asked to say and do to keep the peace. So much I was asked to forget.

The Shaneé who was trying to be the perfect daughter with the perfect life was never treated like a burden. But the real me *was*. The me who fought anxiety about my body every single day, who felt my body was my enemy, who was convinced this was all my fault. The me who had been told how to feel and what to say to those I loved the most by the ones who supported me financially.

I didn't yet know that, years later, psychologists would discover that "invalidating environments"—environments where talking about private feelings and experiences is met with correction, punishment, or guilt-tripping—are one of the top predictors of a child's mental health outcomes.[1]

I now realize that the "me" who wasn't a burden and the real me weren't the same person. That was why I felt the way I did. The message I got was that the "me" who wasn't traumatized, who nothing bad ever happened to, was never treated as a burden. But the me who had feelings nobody wanted to deal with, the me who manifested in my very body turning against me—she sure was. She was the one who I felt, really, none of the people in my life wanted around.

In some ways I cannot blame them. They wished the bad things had never happened to me. When they wished the real me away, what they meant was: "We wish that hadn't happened, so can't you be a version of you to whom it didn't happen? Can't you erase this awful thing, make it so it never happened, since none of us can undo it?"

Nobody knew, when I was growing up, that emotional support might actually be *more* important than financial support to a child's success. In my community, for generations we had been

---

1. *What is an invalidating environment?*. Boston DBT Groups. (n.d.). https://reneehoekstra.com/what-is-an-invalidating-environ ment/#:~:text=%E2%80%9CAn%20invalidating%20environ ment%20is%20one,often%20punished%20and%2For%20tri vialized .

taught the exact opposite. We'd been taught that children must be raised to think and feel "correctly," to express the "right" emotions and hide away the "bad" ones. They'd been taught that this was how they served us: by molding us into what society wanted us to be.

Except that society isn't even what it wants *itself* to be. So how can our honest reactions to it be more "correct" than society itself?

I realize now that *that* is why I'm still here. To help people put words on what they have not been allowed to express. To help people move through the painful process of telling the truth and step into their own power. To drag out into the light that which everybody has tried to hide, because you can't fix a thing by hiding it.

I spent my life being told that I had "wine taste with water money"—that I wanted too much, expected too much, needed to stop dreaming so big and accept that I wasn't the sort of person who got to change the world. The "correct" thing for me to expect was an ordinary life—a life of silence and conformity.

Well, I got told wrong. I *was* here for a reason, and it wasn't to just graduate college or keep my mouth shut. God made his opinion of that very clear.

He's also made clear his opinion on water and wine: that scarcity is a lie, emotionally and materially. That the water that falls from the sky can be turned into rich, luxurious wine through Him.

Throughout the course of this book, we'll turn water into wine together. We'll do exercises to expose the lies that are holding you back and the truths that can move you forward.

Most importantly, we will see each other. And we will validate each other. And by seeing each others' real selves, by saying "I see you. You are real. I know who you are," we will begin to heal the wounds inflicted by a world which, too often, cannot look the truth in the eyes. And we will step into our power together.

***

Let's take a moment to think about the destination you would like to reach at the end of your own journey. So I encourage you now to dream big, not paying attention to what feels possible or "reasonable" to you. This book is all about expanding your self-belief and your abilities, so start with your dream life.

What are your dreams, goals, and desires? Dream BIG—whatever you dream, I promise there is a series of steps you can take to achieve it if you want to. And in this book, we will focus on giving you the confidence to start undertaking those steps.

Now is a good time to open the companion journal to this book if you have it. This journal will provide some additional in-depth questions to help you along your healing journey, as well as more space in which to reflect on your own thoughts and feelings. If you only have the memoir, we will go through a shorter version of these questions.

In this book, we will trace my journey from a place of hitting rock bottom for the second time to a place of standing in my power and working to uplift other women. Let's take a moment to think

about the destination you would like to end up at at the end of
your own journey.

1. What is the ideal career, relationship, or lifestyle you desire? Describe as many of these desires as you like, and stop
   when it feels overwhelming.In my perfect life, I want:

2. Read over your answers to the last question. How does it
   feel? Is there any part of you that feels bad or frightened
   for asking for such big things? Do you feel excited by
   the possibilities? Do you feel *both* things? Try to fill a
   whole page with your thoughts and feelings. Your feelings
   are important, and they warrant being written down and
   studied, even if you are not sure what to write. Stop when
   you feel exhausted.

When I think of my dreams, I feel:

3. Read over what you wrote. How do you feel? If you feel guilty or ashamed of your desires or if you feel you dreamed too big, do you think you are being fair to yourself? We are often harder on ourselves than we ever would be on other people. What would you say to another woman if she expressed the same feelings to you? Would you say that she deserves to have what she wants? Would you encourage her that she deserves these things and is capable of having them?

If I met myself on the street, I would tell myself:

4. Read over your answers to the last several questions. How do you feel about accomplishing your dreams now? What do you think is needed for you to accomplish your dreams? Is it an internal sense of deservingness? A sense of your own competence? Or do you feel ready and raring to go, but you may need some specific knowledge about business, finance, relationships, your chosen craft, or something else in order to begin meeting the concrete milestones that will get you there?

To reach my dreams, I need:

5. In addition to our desires, it is important that we live in accordance with our values. If we are not clear on what our values and principles are, and what kind of difference we feel called to make in the world, we may end up feeling unsatisfied even if we get everything we thought we wanted.What are your core values? Identifying your core values sets the foundation for your expectations. What are the principles that guide your life? What matters most to you? What kind of difference do you want to create in the world?

6. Read over your writings so far. You're a pretty impressive person, huh? What do you think of yourself now that you see your dreams, desires, feelings, and values laid out on paper?

Psychologists say that we fall in love with people when we learn intimately about their desires and their pain. When we fall in love with someone, we want to take care of them, protect them, and advocate for them. We want to help them achieve their goals. I invite you now, and give you permission, to fall in love with yourself.

How do you feel about yourself now, after reading your own intimate thoughts and feelings? How would you like to take care of yourself moving forward?

Chapter Two

Shhh...Our Little Secret...

I was raised by a village. I had a mom and dad who split when I was small, but each still wanted to be around *me*, so my dad flew me out to California whenever I was on break from school, and he could get a break from his job with the airline.

My mom and I lived with my Granny for most of my childhood. There were always people at my Granny's house; family, and friends who were considered family. Aunts and uncles were practically like second parents and cousins were practically siblings. People came and went as they pleased, watched, and disciplined each other's children.

Sometimes I would go with my Granny to cook and clean for one of her best clients, Mrs. Mason. Mrs. Mason didn't mind having me around while Granny scrubbed and swept and would even give me candy because I was well-behaved.

When I was very small, one uncle was particularly close to my heart. Uncle J.P. was Granny's firstborn son, but he looked much younger than his true age. Everybody sort of knew he was an alcoholic, but he took his duty to protect his family as a solemn oath. My mother trusted him implicitly, and rightly so. She'd leave him in charge of me when she had to leave for work.

He never touched a drop of alcohol while I was with him. He was a gentle giant and a watchful protector. I'm quite sure he would have beat up anyone who hurt my cousins or me. Even around the house he stayed sharp-eyed, sometimes squinting into the corners to make sure there was nothing there that would harm me. I guess he'd seen some things in his life. And he gave the best hugs.

When my mom came home, he'd go out and live his life. That was the understanding: nobody could control what he did out there, or tried to, but he never brought anything home that could pose even the slightest risk of harming us.

To this day, his scent—a blend of something sweet, maybe rum, with cigar smoke and a hint of musk and violets—hits me in the heartstrings like a gut punch. He was the first close relative I can remember dying, when I was five years old. It was liver failure, almost certainly. I remember his eyes turning yellow. And I remember trying to get into the casket with him at the funeral, trying to climb inside and for one last hug.

I realize now that he means so much to me because he was my protector. When he was around, I always felt a deep sense of safety, certainty, and warmth. I knew nothing bad could happen to me while Uncle J.P. was around.

My cousin, though. My cousin was another matter.

Jasper (not his real name—no good would come of sharing that now) was probably about twelve when I was four. Old enough to have needs that a four-year-old knew nothing about.

"Let's go play doctor," he'd suggest when he was over, and lead me to the laundry room out back.

It was normal for all the kids, nearly a dozen of us, to play together outside unsupervised. And it was normal for little kids to do what older kids said. Jasper was old enough that he was sometimes put in charge of keeping us younger kids in line, of making sure we were doing what we were supposed to be doing.

This didn't feel like something we were supposed to be doing. But how does a four-year-old say "no" to a twelve-year-old? Especially when she's never been taught that it's okay to say "no" to anyone about anything? That was the standard education back in the day, and it still is in too many places. You're always obligated to do what the "grown-ups" say, no matter what. Grown-ups are always right, and you, a little kid, are always wrong. Even if it's another kid your age, you're supposed to be "nice" and accommodating, especially if you're a girl.

Even when they want to touch your body.

Jasper knew that four-year-old me wasn't going to say "no" to him. He knew I wasn't going to tell. Telling on an older kid fell into a sort of weird gray area of kid ethics: they were old enough to be practically grown-ups, whose bad side you didn't want to get on, but also young enough that you felt some sense of solidarity. If you did successfully get them in trouble, there would be *guilt*.

The abuse followed the regular pattern. Once he'd done it to me once, and I had the strong sense that it was wrong, it was easy to get me to keep my mouth shut. "You'll get in trouble," he'd warn me, "for letting me do it to you. No one will believe you didn't want it. No one will believe it wasn't your idea."

Other times he'd try to coax me: "Don't you want to make me happy? This makes me happy." "This is a really fun game. Don't you want me to have fun?"

Sometimes I'd hide from Jasper, burrowing under the black plastic trash bags full of things that had been put away for storage in the laundry room when he was over and praying that he wouldn't find me. I remember my tiny heart pounding with fear when he'd open the door. The door would creak eerily as he opened it, and his footsteps echoed in my ears as he slowly walked around the place, looking behind things for me. I would have to stay perfectly still and silent if my attempt was to have any hope of success.

Somehow, no one ever noticed that the oldest boy and the youngest girl would often disappear together. None of the other kids ever asked where we were, and if any adults did he always had an explanation ready.

When Uncle J.P. was watching me, it wouldn't happen. I would stay close to him, and he wouldn't let me out of his sight. But if the grown-ups shooed us outside so they could have grown-up conversations, or if cousins came over and it would be "rude" if I didn't play with them, Jasper would find me. And I didn't feel like I could say "no" to someone who was practically a grown-up, who had threatened to get *me* in trouble by telling if I didn't do what he wanted.

After Uncle J.P. passed, Jasper got bolder. That was his undoing. He would grope me when other people were around, or put my hand in his pants when we were strapped into the back seat next to each other if he thought no one was looking. This went on for years. No one ever noticed. I just had to sit there and act normal, acting "okay" with it all while keeping my mouth shut.

One night when I was eight and Jasper was sixteen, my mom's shift at work was changed at the last minute. She didn't go in to work at the night shift like she usually did. She and I shared a bed. Jasper didn't know she hadn't gone to work.

Jasper crept down the hall from the living room where he'd been lying on the couch. He army-crawled along the floor as he approached my room, to avoid being seen by Granny or any aunts or uncles or cousins whose doors might be cracked as he crept past them.

He stayed low to the ground as he crawled right up to my bed, unbuttoned his pants, and reached up under the covers. Normally, he'd slip his fingers under my underwear and start to slide them down towards my knees.

This was how he missed the fact that my mother was in the bed with me. This time when he reached his hands under the covers, it wasn't me he felt. It was my mother.

Being groped by a strange pair of hands while you're lying in a dark, silent room in bed will get your attention real fast. My mother jumped out of bed, turned on the light, and saw Jasper crouching on the floor with his pants unzipped, staring up at her with wide eyes.

She had to know why he was here. He'd come for *me*.

She screamed. And then she was screaming questions and accusations, and Jasper was frozen in fear, and every light in the house was on as relatives rushed in from all around to see what my mom was screaming about.

I remember the scene like a snapshot in my mind. Jasper on the floor with his pants unbuttoned, staring up like a deer in headlights. Granny and my uncles charged in, one behind the other, in a matter of seconds, blocking the door. Everyone was staring at Jasper and shouting as my mother berated him.

But also in the middle of the picture was me, eight years old sitting on the bed with my back against the wall, probably just as scared as Jasper was as the adults yelled.

I believed him when he said that no one would believe I didn't want it. I believed him when he said I'd be in trouble too, that I'd be blamed for not stopping him from doing what he did to me. I believed him when he said that this was *both* of our problems, that it was my fault too, that I needed this to be kept a secret as much as he did even though bringing it out into the light could make it stop.

There's a reason that these kinds of lies worked back then. There's a reason victims were afraid to come forward. It took less than fifteen minutes for the grown-up's angry eyes to turn to me.

"How long has this been going on?" My mother demanded. "Why didn't you say anything?"

"Why did you let him do this to you, Shaneé?" An uncle exploded at me. "Why would you think this was okay?"

Why is this my fault? I wondered, trying to shrink into the bed and disappear.

Jasper was hauled to his feet, and he was punished. Even though my mother yelled and fought for me, the decision the family reached was that no one was to be told about what he had done. It was never to be spoken of again. The way my family and many others in the Black and Brown communities saw things, there was no way to undo it and no way to fix what had happened. If we couldn't make it so it never happened, the next best thing was to *pretend* it never happened. Out of sight, out of mind.

"We can't go to the police," I remember Jasper's father arguing at a tense conversation in Granny's living room. "It would ruin his life."

Everybody just expected *my* life not to be ruined. And it was my job to live up to that expectation.

***

We are beginning this book with the heavy lifting. With the parts of our lives that we do not *want* to look at. I could have told you first about my victories, or even my more socially acceptable traumas, the kinds we have support groups for because they are tragic but not taboo things that happen to adult women and which most people are comfortable publicly supporting someone through.

But that would not have been the whole story. It would not have been the real story. It would not have explained the nagging self-doubt and discomfort with my beautiful body that I felt when I walked across the football field as Homecoming Queen. It would not have explained why I felt inadequate, somehow *wrong*, even as I won popularity contests. It would not have explained why I tried to kill myself twice in my first five years of adult life, the constant battle with self-sabotaging, or why at some level I blamed myself for my breast cancer scares and my miscarriage.

So often, the things that hurt us are done out of love. In my family's case, they thought the best way to erase what had happened to me was to pretend it had never happened. You can see the abstract logic of this. This might have been the best option for previous generations of my family had, when our ancestors had no power to bring abusers and oppressors to justice and attempts to do so might have brought more violence down on the family.

But this is why it is wise to constantly reevaluate our changes. Almost all "maladaptive" responses—responses that don't help us, or that make our lives worse—have developed because they were useful at one time. But we don't live in the same time now that we did one year, ten years, or one hundred years ago.

So we must ask: what is no longer serving us? What can we do better now that might not have been possible before?

I believe that these early childhood events shaped my early outlook on life so much, precisely *because* we did not talk about them. The problem was not just that I was touched inappropriately and against my will: it was that my family's response to this, society's response to this, was to hush it up, to pretend it never happened, while making me feel bad that it *did* happen and for having feelings about it.

The larger problem was that my understandable, unavoidable feelings of fear and insecurity and shame were treated as *wrong* by the world around me. Therefore, *I* was wrong, there was something wrong with *me*, because I didn't feel the way everybody expected me to as they expected me to carry on my life without support or validation or being allowed to publicly grieve for the loss of my innocence.

I became so good at masking my feelings: looking fine on the outside, but slowly dying on the inside.

It's the traumas we don't talk about that make us feel like we don't fit in. It's the emotions that we are told are wrong, are too much or not enough or not appropriate to be discussed, that get stuck in our bodies and fester there. It's the ways in which our inner world does not match what people expect us to be that leave us feeling "I am wrong, inadequate, a disappointment."

In this book we will uncover the healing power of truth, the healing power of painful conversations, and the ways in which *avoiding* pain is often the worst thing you can do for yourself or others.

But for now, to find what's holding us back, we've got to find the things we haven't been allowed to talk about. And talk about them.

In the journaling questions below, I invite you to think and write about the things that have happened to you that you have felt you weren't allowed to talk about. I invite you to find a therapist or counselor, a support group, a book club, and *talk about* your unspoken truths together.

As you talk about these things in the sight of your sisters, you may find that you feel parts of yourself becoming illuminated, becoming real, that have previously felt like dead weight hidden in the shadows.

You may find that parts of yourself you have assumed are bad, worthless, unworthy, suddenly begin to look strong, admirable, and useful once they are dragged out into the light.

You may find that you are becoming more whole, that what you thought was inadequacy in you was actually you holding much of yourself back from the world because you thought the world didn't want those parts of you.

So let's talk. Tell me:

1. What was something that happened to you when you were little that you didn't feel you could talk about? Have you felt you couldn't talk about it because you felt it was "your fault," or because you felt it "wasn't important?"

2. How do you think this event changed you? Is there a fear
   you developed because of it? Is there something you don't
   do anymore, or are afraid to try, because of it?

3. How do you wish your family, or the other adults involved, had handled this situation? What would you have
   asked them to do if you felt you were allowed to ask for
   what you needed?

4. Now, what do you want to tell the world about this event?
   What do you want people to know about how it affected
   you, and how you wish they would handle it if something
   similar happens to someone in their life?

5. Now that you have had the moment to reflect, what is something that you have accomplished or can give yourself credit for doing despite what has happened to you?

You can repeat these exercises with different life events as often as you need to. I do encourage you to find a real-life community of people you trust to do these exercises with. It may be helpful to find a community of people who have experienced and overcome what you've experienced.

The power of speaking your truth out loud, and being seen and validated, is transformative for all involved.

I am also a huge advocate for therapy, and I highly recommend finding a therapist who you connect with and trust. Therapy has helped me tremendously on my journey, as you will soon learn. It's not just for "bad" moments in our lives.

Chapter Three

The Rollercoaster of Emotions

I n high school, I was what I call a "tomgirl." I dressed casually and conservatively. I wanted to be as stylish as possible with the clothes my family could afford but didn't want to show off my curves too much, for reasons that I tried not to think too hard about.

When I did wear form-fitting clothes, I was very self conscious of the fit, how much the outfit showed, and where I wore them. If you paid close attention, you'd see me tug here or pull there. When I was playing sports I convinced myself that I couldn't be held responsible for our uniforms. If I was at home lounging around with people I trusted or felt comfortable around, my anxiety eased, but I still judged my clothes and how they fit in my head.

We still lived in a culture where we were expected to be pretty and feminine, but simultaneously shamed and blamed for it when our bodies "made" boys mistreat us. And I had too much firsthand experience with that.

My anxiety about sex and puberty were high. At home we weren't even allowed to *talk* about sex without getting dirty looks. School bombarded us on every side with information about sexually transmitted diseases and the risk of pregnancy, which most forms of contraception could not completely eliminate. I imagined getting some incurable virus if I ever had sex, even against my will. I imagined having my entire future shot if I came down pregnant before I was able to graduate college and get a job that paid a living wage.

I got my first period at 12, while cheering in the middle of a basketball game. Which was every bit as embarrassing as you might imagine. My mother then deemed that it was time for me to visit a gynecologist for the first time.

This did not go well.

Fortunately, I didn't have any flashbacks as the female doctor looked between my legs. But the comments she made set off a firestorm since my mother was still in the room.

"It looks like your hymen isn't intact," the doctor murmured as she examined me.

"What?" My mother was instantly on high alert, spearing me with a piercing glare. "You're having *sex?*"

I could feel the steam of an epic blowout gathering.

"No!" I howled in protest. "I didn't—it's not—" I stared at my mother desperately, unsure how to *remind* her that I'd been raped by a family member many years ago, especially in front of the gynecologist.

She was about 90% of the way to a full-blown meltdown when she appeared to remember.

The doctor continued her examination.

"Hmm..."

I squirmed.

The doctor was frowning now, and it didn't look like just confusion.

She withdrew and straightened up, removing her latex gloves.

"So you say you're not sexually active?" she asked me.

I shook my head frantically.

"We should probably get you in for a pap smear anyway," she murmured. Then she paused and sat down, putting on her 'we need to have a serious talk' face.

I sat up and swallowed, my heart pounding.

"Your cervix is tilted at an unusual angle," the doctor explained. "This might make it...difficult for you to conceive children in the future."

My heart jumped into my throat, then. I didn't want kids *now*, or any time soon, but someday...

I felt my eyes start to fill with tears. I looked to my mom for support, and she was looking at me like she didn't know how to feel. I guess it was a lot for her to process. She made a gesture with her mouth and nodded at me, it did give me a sense of relief that she wasn't angry or disappointed in me.

We went home, and I kept quiet about that just like about everything else. We didn't really talk about sex, besides "don't do it until you're older" and "stay protected when you eventually do."

I was crushed, because I had the dream of one day being a wife and mother. But I changed the subject in my mind because after all, I shouldn't be thinking about having kids any time soon.

And worrying about it, I was told, wouldn't make it any better. There wasn't any point to talking about what you couldn't change.

***

My first year of high school, I watched the cheerleaders perform astonishing feats of athleticism on the field. I was positive I could never become one of them. They soared through the air, did back-flips and handstands all with a confidence I could never imagine possessing. I couldn't compete with the girls who I saw audition-ing for the squad, so I signed up for the color guard instead.

Color guard was its own kind of athleticism. We didn't have to be as nimble or as flexible, but we had to be *strong* to spend hours practicing with our heavy flags. The flagpole had to be heavy enough to counteract the drag from wind resistance that the flag encountered flying through the air, and we had to fight the weight *and* the wind resistance to execute our synchronized routines.

I once heard a story of a man who made the mistake of trying to assault a girl walking home from color guard practice. You *definitely* don't want to be hit by a color guard's flag, anymore than you want to be kicked by a ballerina. Executing those graceful movements requires tremendous power.

There is a reason we're talking about this, I promise.

After a year of color guard, my physical confidence was boosted. I felt stronger than the year before, and more confident in my abilities to execute precise, disciplined synchronized routines with a group. My friends encouraged me to at least try out for the cheerleading team.

To my surprise, I made the cheer squad—and became a flier, which is a cheerleader who is lifted and sometimes thrown high into the air by teammates.

Being a flier is challenging. It takes a lot of work, trust, body strength, and focus to stay up there. Most people just look at cheerleaders and think it's easy or "not a real sport," but *au contraire*.

If a color guard must have strong arms, a flier must have a strong core. As a flier, you *become* the flagpole. You've got to stay strong and straight, and you've got to develop exquisite balance so you can keep your center of gravity steady while you're being lifted into the air with your feet planted in the palms of your teammates' hands.

It's the "bases," the cheerleaders who lift you up, who appear to be doing the heavy lifting. But have you ever noticed how picking up a cat is like picking up Jello or a sack of nails when they don't want to be held, but when they *do* want to be held they're light as a feather? It's like that.

If you try to lift a random person up and have her stand in the palm of your hand, you won't even be able to get her above the height of your shoulders. But if you've got a trained flier, she knows how to hold her body tight and rigid, how to keep her body balanced. If the flier loses her balance and her center of gravity shifts even slightly, there's nothing you can do to keep her in the air with just your two hands.

This is why cheerleading and gymnastics should be considered among dangerous school sports. I stood on my classmates' palms, often six or more feet off the ground on a living balance beam. I was thrown into the air, and we made it look *fun*, but it required precision. Cheerleaders are just as likely to be injured during performances as football players are to get injured on the field. So, when one day I felt pain after I fell back into my backspot's arms, I assumed it was from overtraining.

There are a lot of ways to come out of a flying position. One of them involves a controlled fall into the arms of a specially trained support cheerleader, called a backspot. In one of these falls, she catches you with her arms under your armpits. Because you as a flier are good at distributing your weight, this is not supposed to hurt.

One day during my senior year of high school, it did hurt. As I fell into the backspot's arms, the side of my breast felt sore and tender. I winced and told myself it must have been muscle pain from training the muscles around my ribs.

But then I took a shower. I did a self-exam. There were sore, tender lumps, everywhere, I mean everywhere, in both my breasts.

My heart pounded in my throat as I panicked. I knew all about breast cancer, and I didn't want to die from it. I was already freaked out by the fact that my body was beginning to change.

As puberty hit me, it filled me with conflicting feelings. I could see that my body was beautiful, and that brought me a sort of joy and satisfaction. But that admiration immediately triggered another feeling: a fear of being *too* beautiful, of being too desirable.

I feared actually liking a boy, but not trusting that he would not hurt me. I feared being different from my friends and did things to just fit in so no one would know all of these conflicting feelings I had. I feared attracting male attention, male lust. I feared being shamed and blamed for being *too* sexy whether an assault came from it or not.

I'd had my fill of being touched because boys "couldn't resist." And I'd had my fill of being blamed for his behavior, even for his temptation, of being asked "why didn't you stop it?"

When I was eight, nobody asked me "why were you wearing that?" or "why did you go out with him if you didn't want this to happen?" When I was eight, those questions were obviously ridiculous. But now that I was changing, becoming what society viewed as a sexual being, maybe they wouldn't be.

Maybe if I wore the wrong thing, something would happen or maybe nothing would happen. But I'd be blamed anyway for some boy's hurt feelings or evil thoughts or just because something *might* have happened. And now it seemed my budding breasts were turning against me, filling with painful lumps that could be cancer.

My mother reassured me that it couldn't be cancer. I was sixteen, after all, and led a healthy lifestyle. Healthy sixteen-year-olds don't get cancer, she said. And if it was cancer, how could it be happening in both breasts at once?

But she couldn't explain what it was. And so we went to a doctor, who ordered a mammogram.

The mammogram was the most painful experience of my life up to that point, because of the cysts. Having your breasts crushed between two cold metal plates is not pleasant on the best of days. When you're there because your breasts are riddled with lumps that are painful to the touch, it's excruciating. They kept having to press them flatter, trying to get a better picture, while I squirmed.

The pictures were taken, but there was nobody there who could interpret them right away. I saw the pictures, my breasts flattened out and filled with ominous bright spots that nobody could explain. The techs weren't allowed to tell us anything, and the doctor who could interpret the pictures wouldn't be in until tomorrow. And when she got into the office, she would have a lot to do. We were told to go home and wait for a phone call.

We went home. And waited.

And waited.

I don't know if you have ever waited to learn if you have cancer, but a second feels like an eternity in that situation. This is doubly true when you are a teenage girl who has survived no health scares, whose entire life has measured less than two decades. Each second that ticked by on the clock was thunderous in my ears, as I wondered if my time to live was running out.

They called. And they asked us to come in again. They sounded puzzled. Not grim, at least. But not reassuring either.

At the second appointment, a doctor examined me in-person. I did not enjoy having my breasts examined by a strange woman, especially as she needed to *feel* the sore nodules. But at least she told me what she was doing. At least I knew that it was necessary. She peered at me curiously, like I was something she hadn't seen before.

"We don't quite know what causes cysts like these," she told me, gently feeling the lumps. "They're not cancerous—but we don't know if they might turn into cancer. We'll need to do another mammogram in three months. And as long as they don't change and stay benign, you will need a mammogram every six months."

"Every six months?"

The doctor stepped back and shook her head. "We don't know what's going to happen. There's a lot about the body that we still don't understand. You're fine for now. But we need to keep making sure you're fine. Come back in three months and we'll see how the cysts have changed."

First, I was relieved. I didn't have cancer, according to the official doctor's diagnosis. I'd done everything right, gotten looked at and scanned, and I didn't have cancer.

But I might get it. And when I was done being relieved, I got angry.

Why did my body seem bent on destroying me? First my body had attracted Jasper's attention, and now this?

Since those early days of molestation I had viewed my body, and particularly my curves, with deep suspicion. I knew those curves had something to do with why Jasper did what he did to me, and with why my mom and Granny sometimes spoke with disdain of "hoochies" who tempted men by displaying their bodies too prominently.

There was something inherently dirty and wrong about having a curvy body, according to society. But also you were *supposed* to, and if you had a flat chest or a bulky belly that hid your curves that wasn't right either.

I had gained confidence in my strength, in the power of my body, in color guard and cheer. But my breasts were now confirming that some parts of my body would never be my friends, and they seemed to have it out for me.

***

I did not know, at that time, that scientists would someday find a link between trauma, fear of sexuality, and physical disease.

I *did* know that I, at some level, feared my body. At some level I already felt that I was damaged goods, and that certain body parts in particular were likely to be sources of trouble. A doctor would likely say that there is no direct mechanism for someone not *liking* a part of their body to cause disease in it. But with each passing year we find more chemical links between our emotions and our bodies.

In 2015, "The Body Keeps the Score" by Dr. Bessel van der Kolk popularized the evidence that people with traumatic childhood experiences are more likely to have autoimmune diseases in which the body literally turns against itself, along with the evidence that treating and resolving trauma actually improves these medical conditions.[1] Among other things, the book explores correlations between childhood traumas and the frequency and severity of autoimmune diseases.

I highly recommend this book for anyone who feels limited by childhood trauma, although be warned: it contains explicit descriptions of child abuse in places which can be upsetting. Van der Kolk discusses some of the most traumatized patients he has worked with, and how they became empowered by engaging in activities ranging from psychotherapy to yoga to martial arts to theatre.

Physical explanations for these findings exist. The impact of stress hormones on immune function, the impact of physical trauma on reproductive organs. In recent decades, doctors have learned that stress hormones suppress the immune system as well as growth and healing functions, making diseases and complications of all kinds more likely. They've found that, somehow, through mechanisms as yet unknown, trauma in the body could make the immune system more likely to turn against the self.

The spiritual dimension, in my opinion, cannot be ignored. When people come to see their bodies as the enemy because of trauma, their bodies *can* actually turn against them. I share this not

---

1. A., V. der K. B. (2015a). *The Body Keeps the Score: Brain, Mind, and Body in the Healing of Trauma*. Penguin Books.

to disempower people who have endured trauma, but rather to do the opposite.

If you already have a condition like this, you know about it. And now you know that through therapy, through the healing of your soul, possibly your body can be healed too. You now know that treatment for PTSD can cut levels of stress hormones in half,[2] that anything that makes you feel more whole spiritually really can improve your physical health.

In his book, Dr. Van der Kolk encourages people struggling with trauma and its aftermath to engage in activities that heal their relationships with their bodies, prompt them to develop a sense of physical power, or make them part of a supportive community in which they can play an essential role and feel useful.

I may have lucked out, then. It is possible that my cheerleading activities helped me to see that I could be physically powerful and competent, even when my earliest experiences of my own body were disempowering. It's possible that the volunteer work I began doing at the African American History Museum helped give me a sense of my culture and myself in the grand sweep of history, helped to teach me that abuses were not okay, and I had a duty to right wrongs.

---

2. Pacella ML, Feeny N, Zoellner L, Delahanty DL. The impact of PTSD treatment on the cortisol awakening response. Depress Anxiety. 2014 Oct;31(10):862-9. doi: 10.1002/da.222 98. PMID: 25327949; PMCID: PMC4388208.

I had some amazing people with me on this journey of discovery. They helped to empower me and tell me to love all things that made me unique. I had my childhood best friend, Lasheika, right there with me while I volunteered, learned, and grew. We lived beside each other, and we spent a lot of time together and with each other's families.

We ventured together on our journey of learning about our history and fully engulfing ourselves in the culture we were learning about. We had similar lives, living with our moms, being raised in a single mother household but our fathers were still present, and we were curious about life and learning all we could.

This journey was so fulfilling for us, yet not everyone understood why two young girls were so interested in learning about our history and spending so much time volunteering and giving tours at the museum. We were young, but we were on a mission.

If I had not had Lasheika by my side, I may have given up when I came across the naysayers who didn't like what we were learning about Black history at the museum.

While we were raised very similarly and our moms were strict, she still had a level of freedom she sought and lived by. She wasn't afraid to cut off all of her hair, and did it more than once. There were times when she would sense my uneasiness and without one word, she'd grab my hand and give me a look that said, "I got you." One of those moments came during our rites of passage ceremony.

This ceremony was a loose recreation of African rites of passage into adulthood. To prepare for it we were assigned research, and were then given gifts directly from Africa, along with African names, in the sight of our community at Atlanta's annual Black Arts Festival.

We were sitting beside each other dressed in all white, many eyes were on us, and she sat with confidence and a straight back looking straight ahead. I was a little slouched and nervous, terrified at being the center of hundreds of people's attention. I slowly turned my head to look at her, to gain some reassurance, and before I could turn around, she looked over at me, gave me that look, nodded her head, and I began to sit upright. I don't know if she even remembers this or not but that is one moment that I will never forget.

I truly feel she was Godsent because I needed her in my life at that time. She was more than a friend. She was my sister. We are still friends to this day.

It's crucially important to surround yourself with the right people who have the right mindsets. Mindsets are contagious, and the company you keep can make your outlook better or worse.

In this chapter, I felt many moments of being powerless and also some when I felt powerful. We should reflect on both moments to make sure we are growing and improving.

Let's answer some questions together, to see where we feel powerful.

1. Where in your life do you feel essential? Is there a group, place, or role where you feel you are doing important work?

2. If you haven't already found your "calling" so to speak, what kind of work would feel useful, essential, and meaningful to you? Is there an issue you'd like to take action on, or a problem you'd like to solve? Is there something you'd like to create? If so, why?

3. Where do you feel physically powerful? Are there any activities you engage in that allow you to test and marvel at your body's capabilities? How do you feel after you complete these activities?

4. If you don't have anything in your life that makes you feel physically powerful, what would you like to try to accomplish that would? Do you feel drawn to martial arts or acrobatics? How about dance or yoga? What sport or art do you love enough that it might coax you to become physically powerful and confident?

I encourage you once again to discuss the answers to these questions with your support group. You might be surprised and inspired to hear how the people around you answer these questions. You might inspire someone else by talking about your own experiences!

As we dig deeper and begin to value ourselves more, we radiate that power outward. We can inspire others to do the same. When we value our own work and see how others value our work, we understand what ordinary people just like us can accomplish by God's grace.

Let us step out of the shadows and into the light, embracing the power within. Let us remember that we are worthy of this happy moment, of this success, and being our perfectly imperfect selves.

Chapter Four

Let Your Light Shine

B y the end of high school, I was everybody's friend. I say this looking at myself from the outside in. I was Homecoming Queen, Prom Queen, and voted Best All Around in my graduating class. Those things must mean I was popular, right?

But I didn't necessarily feel it.

I got popular by being nice. I can at least say that. I didn't have it in me to play "mean girl" games. In fact, I'm pretty sure the *reason* I got popular was that I was constantly afraid of people being mad at me. I couldn't stand the thought of someone being mad at me, and I couldn't stand the thought of someone being in pain. Between those two things, I guess I was super-nice to everybody.

No person is perfect, and I had my off days. I fell short sometimes. But I genuinely wanted to be nice to people and make sure I was a good friend. I knew what it felt like to be left out and judged, and I tried my best not to make people feel that way. I felt my failures to do so keenly, even if I was often too shy to say so.

I couldn't imagine *wanting* to make people feel bad to boost my own status, or just not caring how my actions made people feel.

And I guess everybody noticed.

Inside, I didn't feel like "the popular girl" or the girl at the top of the social ladder. Inside, I felt deeply inadequate. I always doubted whether I deserved to be admired, whether I deserved to have nice things.

I felt like damaged goods because of what had happened to me. Because of what I had *allowed* to happen to me. Because I was told that my feelings were inconvenient and I needed to keep quiet and take it both by my abuser and, to a lesser extent, those adults who wanted to sweep it under the rug without "ruining his life."

I just had to just sit there and be okay with it. Because if I had feelings of my own, other people's feelings would get hurt. Futures would be ruined, and other people would be unable to bear the weight of my feelings added to their own. So it was my responsibility to carry all of us, to be what people needed me to be so they could feel okay about themselves.

If I rushed to cheer people up, it was because I thought that if they looked sad, they had to be feeling desperately, unbearably sad, since to me expressing sadness meant you must have reached a breaking point. I knew what it felt like to be ashamed, humiliated, not good enough. And I couldn't stand for anyone to feel that way.

If I accepted every invitation and rushed to be helpful, it was half because I was afraid people would be mad at me if I didn't do what they wanted. I was afraid that if I failed to solve anybody's problems I'd be somehow responsible for the results, never mind whether I had done anything to *cause* the problem. Like too many women I embraced the role of helper so eagerly that there was no room left for *me*. But I was pretty okay with that since I didn't like myself very much anyway.

This combination of empathy and neurosis worked out pretty well, apparently, because by senior year everybody liked me. The jocks. The nerds. The goths. It didn't matter. Whoever you were, I felt that I could identify with some part of your experience. And I wanted you to like me. And I wanted you to like *you*, too.

As with everything else in life, I was desperate to impress people and meet expectations. At cheer camp one summer I tried out and was selected to cheer at the Aloha Bowl in Honolulu, Hawaii.

As it turned out, my family couldn't afford the travel expenses. But the fact that I was selected meant something. It was one of those achievements that can place a student in a whole other tier of existence in the minds of their peers.

But I didn't feel like an overachiever. I felt like I was just barely getting by, keeping the feelings of being not-good-enough at bay.

I loved to wear loose-fitting clothes. When my brother Monta left for the Air Force, I especially loved to wear his clothes. They were roomie and comfortable and did not show my body. I'd find ways to make myself look feminine underneath my big brother's clothes. But my homecoming dress was another matter.

When it was time to strut myself for homecoming my senior year, my friends and family talked me into a form-fitting, burgundy mermaid-style dress. It was probably the most intentionally eye-catching thing I'd ever worn, and even I had to admit that I looked "fine" in it, which was simultaneously gratifying and scary. After all, as a woman I was *supposed* to look beautiful. But I could also be criticized for looking *too* beautiful.

I was convinced at some level that I was doing something wrong by wearing the dress, by doing anything to attract attention to myself. I was afraid that I could be shamed, and blamed, and be called a "hoochie" for it, or accused of acting "better" than I was. I asked my stepdad more than once if I looked like a hoochie, nervously trying to tug the neckline of the dress higher and squirming in an unconscious effort to cover my curves.

"Of course not!" My stepdad exclaimed. "You look beautiful."

People were shocked by how beautiful I was in that dress, maybe in part because they'd never seen me dress like that before. A starlet stepped out where there had been a tomgirl before.

I didn't know what to expect, because the final vote for Homecoming Queen had not been announced. But even to be nominated was an honor.

Stepping out onto the football field with my stepdad at my side was an alien sensation. Moving in the tight-fitting outfit, feeling so pretty but also eager to get out of it.

A part of me still felt anxious and confused: why wasn't I being shamed and blamed for this dress, when girls were shamed and blamed for being desirable all the time? What was keeping me safe here, and how would I know if it changed? I stood in the spotlight loving the glow, soaking in the moment, but also feeling a little bit surreal.

I hope people don't think I'm acting better than them, I thought, as I looked out over the crowd. I could imagine being one of the girls in the shadows, believing I wasn't good enough to be in the spotlight. I had been accused of causing problems for other people *because* I was well-liked before, and I was anxious to avoid that.

"And...the Homecoming Queen is..."

We all held our breaths as the announcement came over the stadium loudspeakers, intentionally drawn out to build the tension.

What would happen if I won? What would happen if I didn't win?

The previous years' homecoming queen was walking towards me. I knew she would keep walking to one of the girls past me. Wait, she slowed down.

"Shaneé Bailey!"

My breath caught in my throat. I think I cried. It meant more to me because I hadn't been expecting it, because I was shocked to be given this recognition.

Maybe, just maybe, I was worthy. Maybe I was good enough.

I loved being on homecoming court. I gradually allowed myself to accept feeling beautiful without feeling wicked, feeling loved without feeling undeserving. The rays of admiration gradually warmed my skin, melting my hesitation.

But even as I enjoyed the festivities, it almost felt like I was phasing in and out of my body. One moment, I would be here basking in the warmth of my peers' affection. The next I would be someone else, certain that I wasn't good enough, that this beautiful person in the burgundy dress must have been someone different. Not me.

I had no problem believing in others and their abilities. The problem I had was believing in me. I must have done a good job hiding those feelings, because my peers didn't seem to see me as an insecure or anxious person. But I would hint at my fears to my mom and stepdad.

Their mixed responses when I shared my dreams and ambitions often confused me more. They would encourage me that I could do things, but in the same breath advise me to temper my expectations. It was like saying "you can do it" in one breath, and "no, you can't" in the next.

One saying that my stepdad used to say about me was that I had "wine taste with water money." The message I got consistently was that I could do things—but not big things. I mustn't get my hopes up too high, and I must always remain cautious. My position was never secure enough to take risks. I guess that was how they felt about their lives, too.

My mother, for her part, was worried that I would be judged as conceited because I had light skin and curly hair, and so she warned me against "acting like I was better than others." These warnings were intended to teach humility and protect me from judgment and rejection, but they came from the days when confidence in women and children was often read as arrogance.

Being ambitious about my classes and my future career was great, but studying abroad was a bridge too far. They believed I could be on the cheer squad when I tried out but cautioned me to avoid setting my expectations too high, and told me that I would have to do it while also working to earn money.

And why did they do this? Not to be unsupportive or mean but because that was how they were raised. And that's how their parents were raised. That's all they knew. That was all a part of the generational and societal cycle.

Winning the homecoming court election created a new complication. My dad was unable to come to Georgia from California for the evening: he wasn't able to get off work for it. If this made me sad, it made my stepdad furious that I wanted to make sure I still respected my dad even though he wasn't there.

At some level I think he always felt he was competing with my father, competing to *be* my father, feeling that my real dad wasn't there for me enough. And he sometimes seemed frustrated that I didn't see it the same way.

When the homecoming court announced me as appearing with my "father," I squirmed. This was not my dad: my dad was far away in California. This was my stepdad, who would never replace the real father I loved. So when it came time for the local newspaper to publish the article about my win, I specified for the reporters that it was my *stepdad* who had walked out with me, not my father, and that that was how I wanted them to report it.

My stepdad felt hurt about that, and he didn't do a very good job hiding it. He felt he'd done more for me than my dad had, and that I should love him more for it.

My stepdad was no villain. I did love him. For many years we had a good relationship. He taught me how to drive a manual transmission car, how to ride a motorcycle, and I could talk to him about anything. And I do mean anything. I loved fishing, riding four-wheelers, and even cutting grass with him. We would spend hours watching movies and TV and cracking up together. He made that "tomgirl" side of me so happy.

We had an amazing relationship. Until we didn't anymore. A day came when I could see a change in his feelings, in the way he spoke. At first I thought it was all in my head. But one day I saw the way he looked at me, and I realized things would never be the same.

Maybe it was because I was growing up. Maybe he was afraid of losing me as I became a woman instead of a little girl. Maybe my growing up wasn't going the way he had expected. I don't know. But somehow I had become, almost, an enemy. Almost a rival to him within the family.

I did my best to preserve our relationship because I *loved* how happy he made my mom. In the years before my stepdad came along, she hadn't been nearly so happy. After all she had been through, she deserved all the love, laughs, hugs, and the places they went together.

She deserved this. I was not going to be the reason it ended. And so I did everything I could to avoid open disputes with my stepdad, to avoid doing anything that might put my mom in the position of having to take sides.

Again I felt that my emotions were a burden, that expressing the way I really felt was wrong. Hurt that I still held a place of honor for my father. I had the feeling that he felt he'd done more for me than my dad had, and that I should love him more for it. Even as homecoming queen, I'd confirmed that my true feelings weren't right.

I think a lot about those girls who everybody thinks have the perfect life, and then later on they try to kill themselves and everyone is surprised. It must be hard to understand, from the outside, how someone can have things you want, like popularity or beauty or good grades, and still be depressed.

I understand exactly how it works. It happens when we don't give ourselves credit for our achievements, when we still feel like we're wrong no matter what we do. We can have succeeded in many ways that other people envy, but still feel deep down that we have failed.

I find that most women do this to themselves sometimes. We often don't let ourselves take credit for our achievements. Even when we're standing in the spotlight, we may tell ourselves that this is just by chance, or that we do not really deserve it, or that even though we've won the highest honor we *still* should have done something different, something better.

Worse, we may take the times when somebody else gets the spotlight as confirmation that *we* are not good enough. And then we are less likely to try to change the world, less likely to let our lights shine, because we are convinced our efforts won't be good enough.

One of my favorite things that my therapist does with me is celebrate my victories. Often we'll be talking about what I think is an ordinary or even an awful day, and she'll stop and point out something I've done that is wonderful. These can be small things ranging from "I said 'no' to something that wasn't good for me" to actually quite big, glaring achievements that I brushed over thanks to my difficulty in feeling and acknowledging my own success.

My therapist reminds me that I was created in God's image, and that I was created with and for a purpose. No matter how good or bad, small or large, God's favor and blessings still cover me.

I want you to know this too! I want you to remember this! I want you to believe this!

Let's feel, acknowledge, and share some victories now. I'd like you to tell me:

1. What is a victory you have had *today*? This can be a small thing, but extra points if you've done something that you've struggled to accomplish in the past.

2. What do you think is the biggest battle you ever won in your life? Do you think your past self gave herself enough credit for that achievement? What would you say if you could visit that past version of yourself now?

3. What victories would you like to lie in your future? What would you like to accomplish that you have had a hard time seeing as realistic? Do they still feel so unrealistic now that you've visited your past victories?

Chapter Five

A New Beginning

S tarting college was an exciting time for me. Not everybody in my family had gone to college, and it was something that we all were determined I would do. I looked forward to my future career as a college graduate. But it was also scary.

I'd always made good grades, but I had test-taking anxiety. That meant I was incredibly nervous about the weight these tests held for my future as I sat down for the SAT and ACT, and the anxiety clouded my brain. My standardized test scores weren't as high as I wanted them to be. They weren't as high as my grades up to that point would have suggested. At the time in the 2000s, nobody was very aware of test-taking anxiety, let alone of racial bias in the writing of tests which is now well-understood.

And anyway, I thought, racial bias couldn't be the problem. It couldn't be the problem because *all* of my friends got into our target school. All except me. And they all decided to attend their dream school.

There had always been an assumption that me and my closest friend at the time would try to attend college together. We'd all assumed that we would get into roughly the same schools, since we had roughly the same grades. When I was the only one who didn't get into the University of West Georgia, that agreement disappeared.

I stifled my hurt and frustration at that, smiling and acting like everything was fine. Like I always did. Like I'd been doing for so long. It had to be my fault I wasn't getting into the University of West Georgia, I told myself. There was something wrong with me. But I had to keep going and meeting people's expectations. So I accepted that I would be attending Georgia Southern University, my second-choice school, on my own.

Like, really on my own. As college announcements came out, I turned out to be the *only* person in my graduating class planning to attend Georgia Southern.

Things immediately got complicated when I started touring the campus. I'd always had a crippling phobia of roaches and other bugs. This didn't affect me as long as I lived in a relatively clean house. But when we visited the Georgia Southern University dorms, there were dead roaches around the dorm rooms, and bathrooms. They said they had just done a big fumigation, which should mean no more pests in the dorms this coming year. But I couldn't take that chance.

These were *Georgia* roaches. For the unfamiliar, these are a tropical variety that are at least twice as big as the average cockroach you see in New York City. Do not Google them if you have a phobia of bugs.

It was all I could do to keep from having a full-blown panic attack as I looked at those roaches, knowing from experience that there were whole *swarms* where these stragglers came from which would probably come out after dark.

I came home shaking. I couldn't live in those dorms if there was even a chance of an insect infestation. I could not. But I didn't have the money to pay for one of the off-campus apartments. So, I struck a deal with my stepdad.

It was important to my stepdad that I graduate from college. Unfortunately, it was also important to him that I let my father know how much he had let me down.

The truth was, I didn't feel that way at all.

I knew my mom and stepdad weren't happy with my dad for their own reasons. They were mad about certain times in my life when he hadn't been there, and I'm sure they had other things to be angry about that they never discussed with me. Like when my dad *didn't* come to see my homecoming court, and I still made sure the newspaper was clear that I was with my *step*dad, who I would not call my father.

What I remembered were the times my dad *was* there. What a close relationship we had when I spent summers with him in California. How much fun it was to be around him, and how much I craved his love. He was always kind to me and showered me with affection when he *was* around, calling me by his pet name for me, "Boo-Bee-Doo."

That was what I remembered. My mom and stepdad didn't come with me on those trips to California. All they saw was the times he *wasn't* there for me, the ways in which he *didn't* support me and that they did. It probably didn't help that my stepdad saw my dad as a rival, not just romantically, but also for my affection.

As mentioned earlier, at one point my stepdad and I had a really good relationship. I loved them both, and I didn't understand why loving one of them should mean *not* loving the other. But over time, I began to sense a change in the family dynamics. The older I got, the more frustrated my stepdad seemed to become that I didn't view him as my primary father figure.

Which was why my stepdad told me he'd pay rent for me to live in a roach-free apartment off campus. But I had to call my dad and tell him how badly he had let me down.

I did *not* want to do this. Deep down inside of me, it felt deeply wrong. I was being asked to say something important, something meaningful, that wasn't in accordance with my true feelings at all. I honestly didn't feel my mother agreed with my stepdad's feelings on the matter either. But asking her to support me in this would put her in a hard place with her husband, right?

Since I was at least four years old I'd been being told to suck it up, keep quiet, and do what my elders told me. I'd been getting told that it wasn't safe to act on my own feelings, that I'd get in trouble for doing so, that it would be more convenient for everyone if I just stopped having those feelings anyway.

And I knew everybody expected me to go to college. The doors of the University of West Georgia had been shut in my face, and

Georgia Southern University's dorms had cockroaches, which I am deathly afraid of to this day. That meant I couldn't go to college at all unless I could stay in an off-campus apartment with no bugs, so I didn't have a crippling panic attack every time I got home or woke up in the morning.

So with tears in my eyes, I sucked it up and called my dad.

"Hello?"

"Hi. Dad."

"Hey, Boo-Bee-Doo!"

I honestly don't remember what I said. I think I blocked it out. My stepdad had given me a list of things to say. A list of times when *he* felt my dad had let me down and not been a good enough father. A list of ways in which he felt that he, my stepdad, had supported me when my father failed.

To my stepdad, this apartment situation was the latest in a long list of failures on my dad's part. My dad hadn't offered to help pay for my college, he hadn't come to my homecoming court. The list went on, going back to alleged failures by my dad that I barely remembered or wasn't even disappointed by, but which my stepdad felt were egregious.

My dad didn't say much as I told him this. That was one of his strengths, in my opinion. He listened to what I had to say, reflected on it, and asked where this was coming from.

He tried to talk to me. I'm sure it caused him pain. And the fact that I was sure he was trying to learn and grow and take responsibility for it actually made it worse.

I was trying to hold back tears by the time I hung up. I was actually angry. I felt almost every emotion you could imagine, but I knew I had to keep them hidden away. I didn't let my stepdad see, or tell him how I felt, because I'd gotten the message about my emotions thoroughly enough.

I think my stepdad thought he was helping me stand up for myself. I think he thought that I was trying to be a good girl and keep quiet when I *didn't* express anger and disappointment with my dad. Since my stepdad felt that my dad had failed me, he thought I must feel the same way. He wanted to "help" me express it. And I didn't know how to say "no" to him. I couldn't afford to anger the person whose financial contribution would allow me to live roach-free while getting my degree.

I had a lot to learn about expressing my feelings. We all did.

It was with a heavy heart that I hung up and started to prepare to go to Georgia Southern all alone.

***

Weeks before school was set to start, a bombshell dropped. West Georgia sent out a whole collection of letters, apologetically explaining that administrative errors had been made during the admissions process that year. As it turned out, I *had* gotten in; I had gotten the appropriate scores and been filed among the "accepted," but the wrong letter was sent to me.

A close high school friend of mine had the opposite revelation. To her horror, she had *not* made the cut for West Georgia, and was only being informed of that now.

She called me up, wanting to talk.

"So..." she hesitated, knowing how it sounded. "It turns out I didn't get into West Georgia. What college are we going to now?"

I tried not to be offended. Told myself that I didn't have a right to be offended that she now expected me to change my plans for her, when she had refused to change her plans to go to West Georgia for me.

"Well, I'm going to Georgia Southern," I told her as calmly as I could. "Where are you planning to go?"

"I...didn't get into Georgia Southern either." She listed off the schools she had gotten into, as though she thought it really was viable for me to change schools now, just weeks before classes started when I'd already grieved the loss of our plans to go to school together and paid a heavy emotional price for my housing on Georgia Southern campus.

"I've already committed to go to Georgia Southern," I told her. "I've signed the paperwork. I can't just pull out on them and tell them I'm going to a different school."

"But...we were going to go to college together."

Where were you when I was terrified? I wondered. I tried to sympathize with her, with how much worse it would have been if I *thought* I'd gotten into West Georgia with my friends and then had it pulled out from under me.

But no one had said a word when they got into West Georgia and I didn't. No one had offered me a word of condolence or encouragement, or even explained to me that they had to take this opportunity. They'd acted as though it wasn't happening, and I had not felt entitled enough to demand that they reconsider.

"I can't change my plans," I told her.

"Shaneé, are you for real?" there were tears in her voice.

The sadder she got, the madder I got. *Where were you when I was sad? Where were you when I was feeling alone?*

"I'm so sorry, but I am still going to go to Georgia Southern." I mumbled. That was the end of the conversation, and sadly, of our friendship.

I had always hated saying "no" to people, and now that circumstances were forcing me to do so, I was *mad* about how much I hated it. I was mad about how guilty I felt for saying "no" to other people, when it seemed like other people had never hesitated to say "no" to me. I now felt guilty about doing the exact same thing that everyone had done to me, making my own decision about where to attend college.

By the time I started college, I was beginning to grow a chip on my shoulder. I felt that I'd been taken advantage of for too long. I had bent over backwards to try to support many people, make them feel good about themselves, do things that they wanted to do even if I didn't want to, and for them to have fun and be happy. Trying not to make people mad at me.

I sucked it up and kept going, but I resolved that I was going to be more careful this time. As I started my college life I told myself, I wasn't going to pour time and energy into being nice and helping people out if they weren't going to return the favor. In fact, I was afraid to be even a little bit nice to anybody, because my experience was that once you started doing people favors, they'd keep expecting more from you.

I was encountering a common problem of people who aren't taught healthy boundaries: since I didn't know how to say "no" to people's expectations, since I didn't know how to ask somebody to leave, I wasn't letting anybody in in the first place. I wasn't going to risk creating the expectation that I might give them what they wanted, because to me building up someone's expectations and then disappointing them was worse than not talking to them at all.

So I didn't help at all, if I could help it.

Inside, I was dying. I was all alone, at this new school, feeling like a failure. My days as a top cheerleader and homecoming queen were overshadowed by the questions of what I had done wrong, of what was wrong with me, and of why I was the only graduate from my high school who ended up at Georgia Southern.

Now, don't get me wrong. I *adore* Georgia Southern today. I have such love and respect for that school. But as a first-year student who had little familiarity with it, whose peers had idolized The University of West Georgia or even The University of Georgia, I couldn't possibly feel that way at first.

I had never really believed that I deserved my high school achievements outside of my good grades, sometimes feeling that the accolades I won must have been mistakes or flukes of random chance. But I was happy to internalize the things I *didn't* achieve as evidence that there was something wrong with me, because that was the message I was constantly getting by this subtle mismatch between how I really felt and how I was told I was *supposed* to feel.

My first year of college might have been the hardest year of my life. I arrived on campus feeling very isolated and alone, miles away from everything I'd ever known.

I moved in with two roommates—sisters, both older than me. Old enough to drink and stay out late partying, and tease me about being a "baby." Their jabs were good-natured, but they were so close, and I was so *not*. I was such an outsider to their relationship, to their entire way of life. Getting to know them better wasn't even really an option.. They were sweet girls, but we just couldn't build a relationship.

And even among Georgia Southern students, I felt like an imposter. I looked at the other students talking and laughing, and assumed that everybody else had *planned* to be there. This was their turf: I was the stranger who was meant to be somewhere else, but couldn't get there.

I was afraid that I'd fail at Georgia Southern but deep down, I think I was just as scared to succeed there as well. I had the lingering feeling that if something good were to happen to me, bad was destined to be right around the corner. It was mentally crippling.

I hid the depression that rippled through my body each day as I walked to class behind a tough exterior. Whenever people asked me for any kind of favor, or even looked at me hopefully, I'd shut them down with an ice cold glare.

No, I couldn't give you a ride to school. No, I wouldn't help you with your homework. No, I wouldn't have coffee with you. Just leave me alone.

I became a "mean girl," not in the sense of playing politics and actively seeking to harm other people, but in the sense of "not having time for any of your bullshit."

I didn't know at the time that this was a common reaction to having been taught that boundaries are not okay, or were "conditional" boundaries. When we're taught that it's wrong and hurtful to say "no" or assert our own needs, we often end up keeping everybody *way the hell away from us,* because to us, having people close means being asked to ignore our own needs and being forced to say "yes" to anything they want.

Years later I would learn how to say "no" without guilt, and find the marvelous freedom to say "yes" that comes with that ability. But when I went to college, my mindset was that I had to say "no" to everything, right from the start of a relationship, or I'd be stuck being forced to say "yes" to a lot of things I didn't want to do.

As you continue to read, I want you to know that I am not placing blame, because we have to take accountability for our own thoughts and actions. But the truth is that there was a constant mental struggle I was fighting, and it was beginning to take its toll.

I bottled it all up, appearing upbeat on the surface while things crumbled inside. Looking back, I realize I was on the brink of a breakdown.

There are so many of us walking around feeling like this today. Sometimes I wonder how many faces I pass by that are masking the same quiet storm within them.

Maybe it's you. Maybe it's someone you know.

***

The purpose of this book is not to place blame. Rather, I think it's important to share how I felt during my lowest moments because people too often feel alone at these times. If there is one thing I hope readers take from this book, it is this: if you are feeling low, you're not alone. And it doesn't mean you can't do anything you set your mind to, even if it feels that way right now.

The questions and exercises for this chapter are a little bit private, for us to reflect on within ourselves. Anyone who wants to, is welcome to share the answers with a support group(s), but you don't have to since these questions are about our inner lives.

This is a good time to practice respecting ourselves by listening to our inner voices about whether we want to share the answers to these questions, or whether we want to pass. It's also a good time to practice respecting each other by honoring and thanking each other for our choices, either to share or to take care of ourselves by keeping silent. Honoring each other's choices and thanking each other for taking care of ourselves are powerful tools that can be used to strengthen each other in any setting.

Now, without further ado, here are some questions for you:

1. Society tells us to measure our success as women in certain ways, especially when we're young. If you're being honest with yourself, how do you measure your own success these days? What makes you feel insecure or inadequate, if anything? What do you feel you must achieve in order to be "doing what you're supposed to be doing?"

2. Who do you think decided how you measure your success? Whose expectations do you feel you have to meet, or who do you think taught you your ideas about what you must do in life?

3. How would you define success for yourself, if there were no outside influences to please? What work would you most like to accomplish, or what would you most like to experience? Does that feel within reach right now, or is it similar to what you're already doing? How would it

change your life if you pursued this work instead of other metrics of success?

4. What makes *you* happy? What are some things that will make you feel fulfilled? At peace?

5. What are some things that you are having a hard time saying "no" to or even saying "yes" to? What are some ways you think you can say "no" or "yes" so you can take control and put yourself first?

Chapter Six

In the Darkness

During college, I met new friends who I was in awe of. I didn't have it in me to be a total loner. I soon met some friends during my second semester on campus.

The dynamic of our friendship reminded me of the popular TV shows that demonstrated how the differing personalities of friends just mesh. It's hard to choose between us being like Joan, Maya, Toni, or Lynn from Girlfriends. Or maybe we're like Khadijah, Regine, Maxine, or Synclaire from Living Single. I think I'll choose The Golden Girls since more people are probably familiar with them.

Tori was short, hilarious, and didn't have time for your drama. She reminded me of Sophia from Golden Girls: a huge personality in a small package, a complete spitfire who wasn't afraid to say exactly what was on her mind. She had this way of saying something funny with the straightest face. She also had no problem with letting you know when she needed her "me time" alone.

If Tori was Sophia then DeAndrea was like Blanche. She was put together, refined, and confident in the way she presented herself to the world. She loved hard, but she did not take anybody's crap. She knew how to gracefully decline an invitation in a way that was impossible to argue with. People treated her politely because it was very clear that no other behavior would reflect well on them. She just projected that aura.

Denise was like Dorothy: not only was she the tallest of us, but she was driven and outspoken too. She always had a way with her words that was smooth as she told you about yourself. She had a snarky sense of humor that you couldn't help but laugh at. Sometimes you may need a dictionary because of the words that she used, and they flowed off her tongue without hesitation.

DeAndrea, Tori, and Denise were so confident, so comfortable, so at ease. They could say "no," kindly and firmly, refusing requests people made of them as though saying "no" was their God-given right. And because they could do that, they could also say "yes" to things without fear of being trapped into an eternal "yes" chain where they felt like they could never say "no" to that person in the future.

"This is who I am," their presence seemed to say. They were unapologetically themselves, and they never bent over backward to accommodate or make others comfortable. They could be kind, deeply so, and helpful. But not in ways that caused them to suffer or run afoul of who they were. They knew how to take care of themselves, and they didn't seem to alienate or hurt people in the process.

How do they do that? I wondered, watching them gently but firmly decline an invitation to a party. *Why can't I do that?* I was in awe of how they stood in their own power, and felt inadequate next to them at the same time. I felt honored by their friendship.

I didn't consider that they might have been raised differently from me. I didn't consider that they might not have been treated like their emotions and preferences were a problem, that it was their job to overcome. I didn't consider that their parents might have taught them they had a right to say "no," that it was important for them to act in ways that were true to themselves and their feelings.

To me, I just saw DeAndrea, Tori, and Denise doing what I couldn't. To me, this was yet more proof that there was something wrong with me.

I often think about the huge gap between how others saw me during this time and how I saw myself. To others, I must have been popular and successful. To be a star cheerleader and a homecoming queen is practically a stereotype of success for a high school girl. In college, I must have been admirable enough that women I admired wanted to be friends with me.

Yet inside, I always felt as though I didn't deserve it. As though any tiny thing I failed to accomplish, or anything anyone did better than me, was evidence that I wasn't living up to expectations. If either of my suicide attempts had succeeded, I would have been one of those girls you read about in newspapers who commits suicide in spite of apparently having it all.

I think about those girls you read about in the papers a lot. I wonder what sense of inadequacy drives all those accomplishments. I wonder what happened to them that nobody knows about. What truths they were trying to run away from. I think of how everyone asks, "How could this happen?" because all they can see is the image those girls projected, not the way those girls saw themselves.

In the early days of my college career, I had not yet found what I was meant to do in life. I was following the path that was laid out for all of us: be a good person, go to a good college, get a good job. We still ranked ourselves in terms of our grades and our social accolades back then. We hadn't yet had the chance to develop our sense of internal mission. Society didn't encourage us to have a sense of internal mission: it encouraged us to be pleasing and profitable, to measure our success in those terms.

I was measuring up pretty well in the eyes of others, but something was missing. Something I wouldn't find, as so many people don't, until I hit rock bottom.

But after a year or so, I thought I had lost that friendship. A mutual friend of ours started a fight over the boy I was beginning to date, who she wanted too. She said some things to me about what I was doing and how I was acting—and she'd heavily imply that everyone in our social group, including DeAndrea and Tori, agreed.

When DeAndrea and Tori would call me after the shouting match, I'd assume that they were calling to yell at me too. I was so used to people being mad at me. So used to affection being fragile.

I stopped picking up their calls, knowing I couldn't handle being yelled at by them.

By my second semester of freshman year before meeting my friends I was a social hermit, outside of going to the RAC, which was the Recreation Activity Center or gym. I was determined to keep my head down and power through the academic work. That was what I came here to do, after all: to make grades, not to make friends.

Then the financial hits started. My part-time job cut my hours, leaving me with virtually no money left over after paying my bills. I applied for food stamps that were available to college students and was awarded a grand total of $13 per month. I began to live on ramen noodles, with juice boxes designed for small children as my source of vitamin C. I was hungry, but I was terrified to call my parents: I didn't want to impose, to make life harder for them when they were already being so generous as to pay my rent.

I couldn't call my dad, either. As far as I was concerned, that bridge had been permanently burned out of my life. I couldn't go off on him like that and then call and ask for money. And that was another reason I didn't want to owe my stepdad more.

The hits kept coming. One of my required classes had mandatory volunteer activities that I couldn't attend due to my paid job. The volunteer responsibilities were often sprung on us at the last minute, and I couldn't just cancel a shift at work to go help out on a show for the school's media department.

Now I had a decision to make: drop or fail the class or miss work and not make money. I was barely making ends meet financially as it was, and the risk of being fired if I missed work was very real.

I was beginning to feel guilty about everything. The guilt I felt over what I'd said to my dad was never far from my mind. Then again, I *also* felt crippling guilt at the thought of standing up to my stepdad. That would have meant putting my mom in the middle of an argument between her husband and her daughter. Would have meant either asking for money while ungratefully refusing his wishes, or not going to college and being a disappointment. I was a horrible daughter, no matter what I did.

I now know that in psychology, this is referred to as a "double bind." When anything you do will be treated as bad and wrong, there is literally no way to win.

My stomach was already in knots about the future as I drove home from class one dark fall day. The question of how I would pay for my future was never *not* on my mind, and the guilt over what I'd done to my father resurfaced repeatedly. To top it all off, I had recently failed an exam, despite being certain I had studied the material in excruciating detail.

It didn't occur to me that hunger and anxiety about my bills could have ratcheted up my test-taking anxiety, sending it off the charts. Instead, I was sure that God was punishing me for being such a horrible daughter. Such a disappointment. And probably for not going to church, too.

Church had always been a big deal to me growing up. Granny was a God-fearing woman who prayed every day, about everything.

Every Sunday they made sure I put on my best clothes and sat in the church praising God.

But as I grew older, my view of the church dimmed. I became old enough to notice when the pastor flirted with women from the church, acting toward them in ways no married man should act toward women under his power.

The pastor started to act like we were supposed to praise *him*, not just God, since he was the one doing God's work on Earth after all. Once he reprimanded me in public for not paying sufficient deference to him when he saw me at the grocery store.

My Granny didn't go to his church, which prompted a tirade from him about how my Granny was going to Hell for failing to praise him as a preacher the next time he saw me.

I also stopped going to his church.

At the time, the decision had seemed perfectly justified. I had no interest in going back to churches if that's what they were like. But the pastor's words still haunted me, sometimes. Especially when I was already feeling guilty over so many other things.

I parked in my apartment complex's parking lot and got out of the car. A strange man shouted at me. "Hey girl, you looking fine! Can I get your number?"

I ignored him, plowing toward the door of my apartment with determination.

"Fine, bitch! You ain't nothin' anyway!" A string of expletives followed, which I will not repeat here.

I got into my apartment and went to the fridge. There was nothing on my side of it except the children's juice boxes. Nothing in my cupboards except packets of chicken ramen. I wanted to scream.

I turned on the living room TV to distract myself. And I wanted to scream again. A Levi's commercial was on. This would not be traumatizing, except it was the *same* Levi's commercial I had auditioned for in an effort to earn the several thousand dollars it was offering to its stars. I had been beating myself up ever since.

Would I have gotten the commercial if I had taken those acting classes? Maybe if I had taken those acting classes, I wouldn't have needed my stepdad's money. Then I wouldn't have had to say those things to my dad. Then I would be able to afford food. Then I wouldn't be such a terrible daughter. Then I wouldn't be such a disappointment.

Watching the happy young people on the screen, reciting the same script I had memorized for the audition, was like a stab in the gut. It was like God was reminding me what might have been, if I'd just made better choices. If I'd just worked harder. If I'd just taken more responsibility for myself.

I'm letting everyone down, I thought, trying to shove the thought of my failed exam out of my mind. *They're paying the rent on this apartment and I'm letting them down.*

I went into my bedroom, closed the door, and sat down at my desk. I stared out of the window overlooking the parking lot.

This could not be my life. I had not worked so hard for this to be my reward. I was not supposed to be the star cheerleader, the great student, the homecoming queen, the prom queen, the happy daughter, to end up subsisting on ramen noodles for $13 a month while I failed exams and tried to figure out how I could afford to pay my bills and graduate.

My mind went to the medicine cabinet in my bathroom. There were muscle relaxants in there from a previous cheer injury. A whole lot of them. I'd been told to be careful not to take too many, because they'd stop your breathing.

If I stopped breathing, I figured, everybody would be better off. They wouldn't have to pay my bills or deal with my inconvenient needs and emotions. They could all just move on and not have to worry about raising and supporting a failure.

Psychology researchers say that women choose suicide by pill so often because they don't make a mess for somebody else to clean up. That's probably the same reason I crawled into my bedroom closet and shut the door behind me after taking them. I wanted to leave behind as little clean-up as possible.

I sat in that dark closet, crying. My tears were hot on my face. I cried so much, my shirt was wet.

I'm sorry, Lord. I know I'm going to Hell, but at least no one will have to worry about me anymore.

And then I was sitting bolt upright, my back straight against the wall of my closet. My head hurt worse than anything had ever hurt in my life, and my shirt was soaked through.

Did I cry that much?

Then the smell hit me. That wasn't tears: that was vomit.

I staggered out of the closet and looked at myself in the bathroom mirror. My face was beet red and I was covered in half-digested pills. I threw up again, this time into the sink. I already felt so sick that I didn't want to take anything else, but I wanted it to be over. I took off my vomit-covered shirt and fell into my bed.

A few hours later, I woke up.

It was dark outside my window. From the living room, I could hear the TV playing softly. I could hear my roommates chatting with each other, oblivious to the fact that they had almost inherited the duty of finding my corpse.

Lord, I'm sorry, I pleaded in my heart, rolling over to look around my room. *I don't want to go to Hell. Please help me to stop feeling this way. Please don't be mad at me. Please help me reconnect with you.* I did not promise not to try again.

I think a lot about those girls who kill themselves and wonder what they might have done if they had lived. I think a lot about those girls and women who want to, and I wonder what they'll find if they stick around long enough.

If you or someone you know is one of those girls, please know that you are worthy of life, finding peace, finding joy. I am proof that times get hard, life feels like it is constantly kicking you, but the fight, no matter how hard and long it may be, is well worth it. You will get there.

Please remember that there is hope, even in the darkest moments, that your life is a precious gift from God, and ending it would not only cause immense pain to those who love you, but it would also deprive the world of the unique light that you have to offer.

One of the greatest strengths comes from reaching out for help and allowing others to support you on your journey. If you're feeling suicidal, please reach out to a crisis hotline or mental health professional. There is help available, and you don't have to go through this alone. I wish someone would have told me this when I was in my dark moments.

I see you. I feel you. I believe in you.

***

As my college years continued, I came a little bit more into myself. Tori, Deandrea and I became a posse, and I began dating a guy who didn't know me by my high school reputation. Further from the influence of my old friends and family, I could ask more questions and consider my own answers to them. But I still felt a deep sense of fragility, a deep sense that I was not, could not, live up to people's expectations.

I still didn't quite know what I was doing as far as "being nice." I couldn't stand to see people in pain, but I was still deeply jaded. I still expected people to want and expect more from me than they were willing to give in return.

There were times, though, when I couldn't help reaching out. And in those times, I now realize, I began to see an inkling of my purposes.

One night, I ended up in the emergency room. A group of friends and I had been driving home when we were hit by a drunk driver, totaling the car we were in. While sitting in the waiting room, I saw another patient being brought inside.

It was another college student, and she was sobbing. Really, sobbing. She was rolled over on her side, curled up into a little ball, clutching a plush, purple blanket she must have brought with her from home.

Alarmed, I looked around for clinical staff. She was in obvious pain, but no one was paying attention to her.

"Hey," I said softly, "are you okay?"

"H-he r-raped me," she sobbed.

My blood ran cold.

I knew something about that. In my mind, what had happened to this woman must have been worse than what happened to me, because she was reacting more strongly. But at least, I knew something about what she was going through.

I pulled up one of the chairs and sat by her. I knew not to touch her.

"That's awful," I said softly. Sympathetic but calm. Not upset, so she wouldn't feel like *she* had to take care of *me*. "Do you want to talk about it?"

She turned around to face me, looking at me with desperate red-rimmed eyes. "I d-don't understand how this could happen to me," she sniffled. "I didn't dress too sexy. I didn't even have anything to drink! They told us not to leave our drinks alone, not even when we went to the bathroom. But he still...he just...he was bigger than me," she started bawling again.

I sat frozen. But not with fear. With rage. "I haven't been through what you're going through," I said, measuring my words as carefully as I could. "But I was molested as a child. And I know what it's like to feel like it's your fault. I've dealt with that my whole life. But it's *not* your fault. It was somebody else's choice to rape you. It wasn't because of anything you did."

She gathered up the plush blanket and sobbed into it convulsively for a while, shaking as I said these words.

"I know how it feels," I said softly again. "It's not your fault."

After what seemed a long time, she looked up at me. Her eyes were a little different now. Still hurt, but a little different.

"You know," she said in a small voice, "I feel like you care more about me than anybody in my group of friends, or anybody at this hospital. None of them have been doing anything. It seems like they all want me to just 'get over it.' I've been thinking about—" she stopped then, and looked away, like she'd almost said something she meant to keep hidden.

I've been thinking about ending my life, my brain finished her sentence.

I have no way of knowing, will never have any way of knowing, if that's what she was going to say. But that's what it felt like to me. That's what some deep, dark part of me that I had not yet acknowledged wanted to say.

My story matters.

That was what I took away from that day at the hospital. The idea that just by sharing my story, I could change the look in someone's eyes like that. That she could go from looking desperate and in too much pain to live, to looking still hurt, but maybe even a little hopeful.

That she could say, past tense, "I was thinking about—"

That thought, the thought I had deep down inside, could become past tense just by listening to someone else's story.

Maybe I am here for a reason, my mind whispered.

It didn't whisper very loud, because I still hadn't quite admitted to myself that I lacked a sense of purpose. I still hadn't admitted to myself that living to make good grades, go to a good college, and get a good job wasn't working for me. I still assumed that the problem was *me*, that I must not be good enough at those things since I never felt fully satisfied or proud of myself by achieving them.

That conversation in the hospital felt different. I felt satisfied and really, genuinely useful there in a way I hadn't felt before. For that moment, I felt like enough. I felt like I had done something that I knew, at a deep level, was valuable. Something that maybe not everyone else could do.

But I was too young to pause or reflect deeply on this. I was still living my life as a college student, still following the road map that had been laid out for me. I would still strive to graduate from college, get a prestigious job, and in that I would justify my existence. And in doing what everyone else told me was "good enough," I would find fulfillment.

I had to, right? That was what people did.

On the surface, I had a pretty great life. I attended Georgia Southern, had my girl posse who respected me and wanted me around for reasons I didn't always fully understand. I went home to a family that was supportive insofar as they were paying for my off-campus housing, and they still wanted me to come home to visit.

But all was not well on the home front.

A few months after meeting that woman in the hospital, I drove home for one of our semester breaks. I wasn't quite prepared for what I saw as I pulled up to Granny's house. As I took my keys out of the ignition, I saw Jasper. Long-since a grown adult now, almost thirty. He was hefting a small girl into the air. Everybody was laughing like this was just a normal thing—a cousin playing with his cousin.

I was frozen in place. Images flashed through my mind. The laundry room. Me, sitting on the washing machine. Jasper, his pants down.

I got out of the car and started screaming at him.

"YOU PUT HER DOWN RIGHT NOW!" my own voice frightened me as it tore from my throat, louder and more powerful than I'd ever heard it.

Jasper froze and looked at me, seeming genuinely confused. The children all froze too, and so did the adults. Everybody staring at me. I was being inappropriate, and I knew it. I was acting crazy, and I knew it. But I couldn't stop.

"I better *never* see you touching her again!" I thundered, stalking toward him as the children started to flee. The adults stared. I was vaguely aware that most of the people in the yard hadn't been there the night he was caught, had no idea what he'd done to me. The ones who *did* know seemed especially frozen. Like they didn't know what to do.

"Whoa, Shaneé...chill."

Jasper had his hands up defensively, taking a step back as I stalked toward him. He seemed *scared* of me at that moment. The idea that he could be scared of me, could back down from me, was gratifying enough to snap me out of it.

I stopped where I was. Straightened up. Took a deep breath. Took my little cousin by her hand. Kept my eyes on him with a death glare.

He went inside.

Then, I was able to relax as best as I could after that adrenaline rush.

Everybody else filed inside. Not talking about what had just happened, of course. Never talking about it. Never talking about it. If they didn't want to talk about what Jasper had done, they wouldn't want to talk about what I'd just done either.

I walked inside and joined the family like nothing had ever happened.

***

That was a lot, huh?

Just as in the other chapters, we have some reflecting to do. For these questions, we will focus on what triggers us.

Have you ever been blindsided by an emotion, a sudden storm erupting on the inside of you? Sometimes your heart begins to pound and maybe you begin sweating. It can be a rollercoaster: feelings of sadness, anger, isolation, and tears.

That's a trigger, a whisper from the shadows of our past. Unresolved pain, buried deep, whispers through familiar sights, sounds, smells, or emotions, reminding us of battles fought and wounds left unattended.

One definition of a trigger is "to make somebody feel very upset or anxious by reminding them of a trauma or bad experience." Yes, triggers can send us spiraling, but I feel that there are also positive triggers.

Picture this: you find that old embarrassing photo of yourself. Cringey, right? It may not have been the best time in your life. But then you laugh because look how much cooler and better-dressed you are now.

Sometimes triggers remind us how far we've come, how strong we are. They're like little growth checks, pushing us to see how much we've healed, grown, and evolved.

So when your triggers appear, don't get mad at the emotions they bring. We're designed to have emotions, and there's nothing shameful about that. The Bible tells us that Jesus displayed many emotions like anger, sadness, compassion, and irritation. He cried, and even flipped some tables.

Emotions are a part of being human that Jesus himself experienced. It's how we choose to respond to them that can make us great or not-so-great people to be around.

So let's get into those questions. We will focus on the most trying triggers, which are the "negative" ones and we typically have a hard time dealing with.

1. Think about the most recent experience that triggered some emotions like anger, sadness, fear, anxiety, etc. What happened just before you felt triggered? Was it a specific event, word, or interaction?

2. What sensory details were associated with the trigger? Sights, sounds, smells, or even physical sensations can be clues.

3. Is there a similar past experience this trigger reminds you of? This could be a specific event or a general feeling from your childhood or past relationships.

4. How did you feel in your body before, during, and after the trigger? Did you experience any physical sensations like tightness, tingling, sweating, shaking, or rapid heartbeat?

5. What need might be underlying your triggered response? Do you need safety, validation, control, or something else?

6. Is there anything you can do to remove yourself from the triggering situation? Sometimes, taking a physical or mental break can be necessary.

7. How can you use this experience to grow and become more emotionally resilient? Can you use this as an opportunity to practice self-compassion, learn new coping skills, or seek support from a therapist?

Here are some affirmations that I use to assist me with my triggers when they arise. After reading mine, choose some that you can connect with AND come up with a few of your own.

1. "My body is strong and capable of feeling and releasing."

2. "I am in control of my own thoughts and reactions."

3. "My past does not define me, it informs me."

4. "I forgive myself for my reactions and choose to learn from them."

5. "This trigger is an opportunity for growth and understanding."

6. "This trigger is helping me to identify my needs and build healthy boundaries."

7. "I trust in God's plan, even when I don't understand the path He has laid before me."

8. "I surrender my trigger to God, knowing I am not alone in my struggles."

Chapter Seven

You Can Do It

After that, I kept thinking about how it had almost all ended. There was something else eating me up inside.

I still remembered the conversation I'd had with my dad, two years earlier. Yes, I was angry that my dad had missed out on some crucial events in my life. Yes, I wished he'd been there for me more. But that didn't mean I wanted to call him up and end our father-daughter relationship! If anything, I wanted him more involved and physically present in my life.

I hadn't spoken to my dad since then. I was too scared. I was certain he'd be mad, that he wouldn't want to talk to me. I hadn't done what my dad wanted in that phone call, that was for sure. As far as I was concerned, I'd destroyed his image of me and destroyed our relationship.

This bothered me enough that I confided in the guy I was dating in college at the time about it. Let's call him Luca. Luca and I didn't work out in the long term, but I felt safe with him. Safe enough to open up about what I felt was this horrible thing I'd done, and how if that was the last conversation I ever had with my father I would never forgive myself.

I hadn't told many people about this at all. It was one of the things I kept buried deep inside.

"Call him," Luca said, as though it were the simplest thing in the world.

I blinked at him with eyes red from crying. "I can't just *call* him," I said. "Not after the things I said to him."

I don't deserve his forgiveness, I thought, then stopped the thought, caught it, stared at it. "Yes you can. You're his daughter. I don't want to invade your privacy, but if *I* have to get his number and call him for you I will. I can see how this is eating you up inside."

I blinked again. I wasn't sure I believed that I could just *call* my dad and pick our relationship up again.

But damn, I had to try, didn't I?

It took me a couple of weeks to get up the courage. Several attempts where I'd pick up the phone, start shaking, and put it back down. Luca kept reminding me that I could, and that I *needed* to call my dad. Finally I worked through it enough to dial his number.

Ring ring. Ring ring. Ring ring. I thought my heart would just about stop each time a ring cycle completed.

Ring ring.

Just as I was about to hang up: "Hey, Boo-Bee-Doo!"

I let out a sigh of relief so big it turned into a sob. There was my dad. Cheerful, yet solid. Loving. Just like I remembered him.

I'd expected him to be hostile, angry. I'd expected him not to answer the phone. Or maybe to answer it with a strong sense of disappointment in his voice. I thought he would demand to know what I wanted, why I was calling after how I'd spoken to him those years ago. I'd expected nothing to be left of the love we'd shared before I said those awful things.

That was how I thought about love. As something fragile, easily withdrawn if you ever stepped out of line.

I just cried into the receiver for a while before I could get words out. I think my dad was probably pretty alarmed.

"Hey, Boo-Bee-Doo. Is everything okay?"

"I'm sorry," I managed, my voice cracking. "I'm sorry about the things I said. I didn't mean them. It wasn't my idea." That last part felt like a lame excuse, a shirking of responsibility. But it was also true, and I wanted him to know that.

"Hey, Boo-Bee-Doo," Dad's voice was deep, but also soft and understanding. "It's okay. I know I haven't always been able to be there for you. And I'm sorry about that. People get emotional and say things, you know? It's okay."

I cried harder at that. I was *so* grateful that he still loved me. I'd spent two and a half years thinking I had permanently broken something precious, that I would never get him back. But he was able to accept my feelings—even the ones I didn't really have—with grace and forgiveness.

"I'm so sorry, Dad," I managed.

That isn't all we said. But those are the most important things.

I was learning, in my budding independence, that I needed to guard my mind. That I couldn't keep letting people pressure me into things. I had to take responsibility for my actions, and part of that meant making sure that they were *my* actions. Not the actions someone else wanted me to take.

After the phone call with my dad, I did eventually let my mother know I had spoken with him and re-opened our relationship. Surprisingly, she was supportive of my decision.

I was now living with Luca. My relationship with my mom was still strong, but I was now trying to figure out how to handle my relationship with my stepdad and not make my mother feel like she had to choose between us. I no longer feared my stepdad's anger or felt like I'd be ungrateful for his contributions if I didn't do what he wanted me to. But there was still the part where any time we had a disagreement, my mom could end up being asked to take sides.

When we had holiday or semester breaks at college, I would often go home with Luca and celebrate with his family. We would visit my family, but we didn't stay long. And as I watched our two families on these back-to-back visits, I began to understand why I felt more comfortable visiting his family than visiting mine.

In my family, there were obviously certain assumptions. There were certain thoughts and feelings you weren't allowed to express, because they could be construed as disrespectful or hurtful to somebody else. Peace was kept by way of silence, and discipline was thought to mean that young people shouldn't ever express disagreement with, or hurt feelings toward, their elders. As far as my family was concerned, that was "the way it was done." If young people were allowed to express their feelings freely, they thought, the result would be that the kids would never develop the self-discipline they needed to succeed in life.

Luca's family was different. They had a kind of open communication I had never seen between different generations before. Their children had discipline and knew how to be respectful, but that didn't mean keeping their mouths shut or their opinions to themselves.

I would sit and observe, not being obvious with it, but taking mental notes as I watched Luca, and his sister and cousins speak up and even say "no" and disagree with the elders in their family. Everyone still ended up laughing with each other. It was like the feelings and opinions of the young people were respected even when they didn't agree with those of the elders. And as far as I could see, no chaos or lawlessness was breaking out as a result. In fact, his family seemed to communicate more easily and be able to resolve differences more easily because they didn't keep feelings bottled up inside until they exploded.

Luca looked at me strangely sometimes when I asked him questions about why his little cousins were allowed to say this-or-that, or how his Granny would respond if one of them said something hypothetical or "out of line." But he would answer the questions. This gave me a window into how, maybe, Tori , DeAndrea, and Denise had grown up with such confidence in expressing themselves and enforcing their boundaries.

In time, Luca and I broke up. He was a supportive person in my life for those years, for which I thank him.

***

Speaking up for myself without having to be the "mean girl" was something I was able to witness during college. I went to college with the goal of growing a backbone, not taking crap from anyone, and not caring who I hurt while standing up for myself. At the time, it seemed like an all-or-nothing situation. The attitude I'd grown up with, that standing up for yourself was most often hurtful toward someone else. Meaning that if I wanted to stand up for myself at all, I was going to have to be okay with being hurtful and not letting anyone "run over me".

That didn't last long. That wasn't me. I did care who I hurt. But it took me a while to figure out that I could say "no" without being hurtful. I just needed to figure out how to be confident and true to myself without assuming the worst of people or pushing them away.

Looking back, I feel that college was God's way of putting people in my life who I could witness in their authenticity and see how kindness and authenticity could exist in the same person. I could say "no" or disagree with someone's opinion, and still have people love and accept me without feeling that I was attacking them or being hurtful.

These people became family to me, and through them I was able to see how family did not always have to agree, or even be happy with each other all the time. But a *true* family, whether by blood or not, will love and accept you. All of you!

The next step was to put what I had observed into action in my own life. I needed to take baby steps toward being the person I wanted to be, the kind of person I admired, and give myself pats on the back when I did.

It began with small "no's" at work, like when someone asked me to switch shifts with them and doing so would have interfered with my life. Or when I was asked to do double work in a group project, and I had to ask one of our groupmates to step up or we'd let the professor know that only three of the four of us had contributed to the project. Or when I was offered an alcoholic beverage at a college party and I said "no, thank you," despite the "ahhh come on, loosen up, have fun" rebuttals that inevitably followed.

Was this easy? Absolutely not. Did I always do it? Absolutely not. There were times when I said "yes" or did not defend myself because saying "yes" was a comfort zone for me.

Unfortunately, people-pleasing was a comfort zone that was often harmful to my well-being. That's why it's so important to keep the right people around you. I had reminders, whether I watched Tori or DeAndrea or Denise or Luca gracefully decline something they didn't want to do, or whether they verbally reminded me to stand up for myself. Sometimes they would even stand up for me because they sensed that I wasn't comfortable saying how I really felt. I tried to begin doing the same for myself, talking myself through difficult situations.

If you are going through something where you are struggling to step out of your comfort zone, or just deciding to do something different, here is your green light to do it.

Move forward. It won't always be easy, it won't always happen quickly, but *you* are worth choosing yourself. *You* deserve peace. When we choose to do different things that others aren't used to, it may come with some resistance. There can be resistance from outside forces, and even resistance within ourselves. But that's part of the process. Growth comes with growing pains.

The growing pains of change may be difficult, but they hold the promise of ultimately becoming who God created us to be. Who we are meant to be. Some people may tell us that God only intended us to be obedient servants, but does that really make sense? Would he have made us "in his image and likeness," with the ability to create and judge right from wrong, just so we can do what other human beings told us to do?

For these next set of questions, I want you to really think about your answers. I want you to choose the answers that make you happy, that bring you peace. Don't base them off of what you think others may say or may want you to say.

Some of you reading this chapter may be just fine with saying "no," but these questions are still relevant to you. I want us to think about the traditions that were passed down to us, that we are also passing on to the next generation.

Traditions are not just what we do to celebrate holidays, birthdays, or special occasions. Traditions are defined as, *"...the trans-*

mission of customs or beliefs from generation to generation, or the fact of being passed on in this way."[1]

This chapter highlighted the traditions passed on to me, that belief that speaking one's true feelings could get you in trouble.

I have changed that tradition with my children. We have discussions, and we encourage them to talk to us. They ask why, and if they disagree with us we ask for further clarity so they can think through their thoughts and gain understanding. This is all done in a respectful manner—perhaps *because* we encourage an environment of respect for other's thoughts and feelings, regardless of age or hierarchical status. If anyone's communication crosses boundaries, they understand the consequences. This change was not easy, and it is still a work in progress because it is easy to go back to how I was raised. This is one of many traditions we chose to change when raising our own children.

With that said, take a moment to reflect on your answers before writing them to the following questions:

1. What traditions are no longer serving you? Your family? Your future family?

2. Who benefits from keeping those traditions alive? Who benefits if you change them?

---

1. *Tradition.* Oxford Languages. https://languages.oup.com/google-dictionary-en/

3. If you could create new traditions that are more meaning-ful for you and your family, what would they be?

4. Not all traditions are "bad" or "harmful." Are there tra-ditions in your family that are beneficial to everyone? Is there a way to honor the past while simultaneously em-bracing the potential for improvement on the tradition you would like to improve?

5. Are there any traditions you have witnessed others do that you would love to incorporate into your life and legacy?

While traditions may be rooted in faith, history, and outdated expectations, we are also gifted with the ability to discern their true meaning and impact. When you are comfortable, share these thoughts with your family and maybe even encourage their input on how they think these changes could be put in place.

Don't get rid of everything that connects you to your history, but you can improve on your family's traditions together. Be pre-pared for some pushback as you begin your journey of creating the traditions you would like to have and give others time and space to experience and explore their feelings on these matters. In this way you can help ensure that you will all leave the legacy you would like to leave to future generations.

You got this!

Chapter Eight
Déjà Vu

A s my college years continued, as I mentioned earlier: obstacles kept piling up. It turned out that the broadcasting major I'd originally planned to obtain was incompatible with students who had to work, like I did.

As part of the broadcasting program, we were expected to help out with local media productions and performances. That would have been fine, except that we were often called in to do so at the last minute. That meant trying to get shifts off of our paid jobs on short notice, and anyone who worked in the service industry in the 2000s knows how impossible that often was.

Bosses would often expect entry-level workers like myself to be available to be called in for work shifts around the clock, but from the employee side of the equation, shift coverage and time off were often nonexistent. As a student who was paying my own bills, I couldn't just tell my boss on Tuesday that I had to take Friday evening off of work to cover a requirement my school had sprung on me at the last minute.

That meant I couldn't meet the requirements of my broadcasting major, and nobody seemed to be very understanding about it.

There was no real recognition of the burdens on working students, or the ways in which requiring unpaid labor on short notice could make a program inaccessible to students who didn't come from wealthy families.

There was no culture among employers of promoting education: instead, workers who were enrolled in college were often viewed as a liability since it was assumed that they would quit the company when they graduated anyway. In my case, quitting my job or refusing to commit to working evenings and weekends was not a financially feasible option.

It became clear, then, that I needed to change my major. I chose teaching because that was something else I found fulfilling. The more of what I saw of life, the more I saw the need to change how we taught young people, to teach them not just academic facts, but also how to communicate their feelings and advocate for themselves.

There was just one problem with the teaching major: there was no way I could get in the necessary credits to complete the major with just three semesters left in front of me. I would have to stay in school and take another semester after all of my friends graduated, which also weighed on me because it meant I would be asking my stepdad to continue paying for my apartment for extra months beyond when I "should" have graduated.

I couldn't help feeling like I'd let my mom and my stepdad down when I announced my change of major. My mom, who had been imagining me as a morning news anchor, voiced concern that teachers didn't get paid very much. My stepdad never said anything, but I knew that he wasn't made of money, and that paying for my off-campus housing wasn't easy for him.

When that final semester rolled around, I watched all my college friends graduate and go off to start their adult lives without me. Again. It was like a replay of my high school graduation, when all of my friends had cheerfully gone their separate ways. I was the only one of my close college friends who didn't walk in May of 2005. Even my boyfriend at the time graduated then.

This brings us to me dropping out of school with one semester left. The stresses of attending the school without my old friends, and with cash flow that was woefully inadequate, had become too much. My mom had just had a surgery that turned out to be more serious than I had expected, and it had all become too much.

I moved back in with my mom and my stepdad, and tensions immediately began running high.

The first thing I figured out was that my mom was hurt that I hadn't come home from school to see her earlier. She'd had a surgery to remove uterine fibroids, which I had wrongly assumed was a simple outpatient procedure. I'd come home to visit her for a few hours, but I hadn't taken days off of school to stay at home with her as she requested. Her fibroids had turned out to be serious.. It hurt her that I wasn't there. I hurt my mom, the person who was there for me to the best of her ability and made sure to provide for me. The one time I needed to be there for her, I wasn't. That hurt me that I hurt her.

My stepdad had his own reasons to be salty with me. In college he had tried to help me with my cash flow problems by signing me up for a multilevel marketing company. He'd pitched it to me as a way I could make extra income on the side, but what arrived in the mail was a box full of stuff that I was supposed to learn immediately to help me find a way to introduce the opportunity to my fellow college students.

Now, as you may be aware, college students are not famous for having disposable income. So I was left wondering, *What am I supposed to do with this?*

I didn't like selling things, and I didn't want to turn my social relationships into selling ones.

Now I'm not sure if my stepdad was expecting kickbacks from the sales I made, or if he was just mad that he had spent money to send me a training kit that he thought would solve my money problems and I hadn't made good use of them. Either way, I think he again felt that I hadn't adequately valued his contributions, while I was frustrated with him for trying to push yet more re- sponsibilities on me when I hadn't asked him to get me involved in his sales operations.

This whole experience was one reason I was skeptical of Reco. He was in network marketing, like my stepdad, though he worked for a different company in a different industry at the time. I still just assumed that the instinct to sell would permeate everything he did, and that he would eventually become frustrated with me if I didn't go along with his network marketing plans.

I was still suspicious of Reco, and now I was living at home with my mom and stepdad. At some level they were glad to have me back around, but it felt to me as though the older and more independent I got, the more we were going to clash.

I became a restaurant hostess and then moved up to become a tipped server. I started taking acting classes at a school in downtown Atlanta, never wanting to feel that I'd missed that opportunity again.

But things were about to get weird, in a way I'd never expected.

***

That summer, a couple of my college friends decided to invite me to a cookout. They were friends with this woman who was getting engaged, and the fiancee turned out to be friends with a guy named Reco McCambry.

I've heard Tony Robbins described as a "toothy giant," and that would not be a bad way to describe Reco when I first met him. He was wearing a linen shirt and khaki type dress shorts, and he was all smiles. He clearly thought that he was *so* cool.

To be fair, he was kind of right. But at the time I didn't like him or his cocky attitude.

At first, I thought he was hanging around me and my friends because he liked one of *them*. All of them were more confident and self-possessed, and more generally *together* than I was. At least, in my opinion.

He came over, asked my friend to come outside to talk for a minute, and off they walked. I was used to guys being interested in my friends first and had often found myself assigned the role of "homegirl" or in the "friend zone." In this case, I was fine with that. I was instinctively wary of men who seemed *too* confident, and to me Reco fit that description.

I had no idea at the time that the real reason he'd asked my friend to leave with him was to ask her if I was single. I decided to go to the bathroom, and not come out again until this Reco person got bored and moved on. As it turned out, this did not work.

Knock knock knock. Someone was tapping their knuckles on the bathroom door. "Shaneè?"

"What?" It was one of the friends who had brought me here. They must have gotten worried when I didn't come out.

"You've got to come out here! Reco wants to talk to you!"

"Well, I don't want to talk to him!" I fumed. I was convinced that I knew his type: if a man was very impressed with himself and his job, I was sure he wouldn't treat a lady right. Plus I was not into arrogance.

"Come on! You've got to give him a chance!"

"No I do not."

"Well, he's right here."

"Just come out." Reco called through the bathroom door.

Oh God. My face burned with embarrassment, and I imagine I turned crimson. He'd heard the *entire* conversation.

After many minutes of dodging him, I sighed, resigned myself to dealing with the situation, and came out of the bathroom.

"Hey there, I'm Reco. What's your name?"

"Shaneé."

I was as cold as I dared, which wasn't very cold: I was still a people pleaser, and was petrified of someone telling me I'd been rude or unkind. So I listened patiently as he rattled on entirely too long about his business. His business seemed to be his life, and apparently that impressed some people. At one point his cell phone rang, and he picked it up without even saying "excuse me" to me.

He *did* glance at me in a way that told me he wanted to see how I was reacting. He wanted me to think he was this big, important businessman.

Yawn. I walked away leaving him outside taking the phone call.

By now, the party crowd had thinned and the festivities were winding down.

"Hey," Reco proposed in his deep, mature sounding voice, "we should go back to my place. We can shoot pool and hang out."

Everybody else was excited about the idea. I'd rode to the party with one of my friends and "everybody," wanted to go, so I guessed I had to go along.

The plan was for us to follow him to his house, but he asked for a phone number for each person who was driving just in case we got lost in traffic. I assumed that my friend gave him her number, since she was driving. But on the drive to his house, my cell phone rang. I pulled it out and stared at the unknown number on the caller ID.

"Well we, uh," my friend confessed, staring at the road to avoid looking at me. "I kind of gave him your phone number."

I leaned back in the car seat, closed my eyes, and shook my head. *Oh, great.*

Reco led our chain of cars in his Jaguar, into a newly developed neighborhood and to a big house. Everybody else seemed impressed, but I was concerned. How the hell was a young man of his age affording a house like this? Was he selling drugs or something? Did he really own a legit business?

We all got out of our cars and went inside, where I saw pictures of a woman plastered all over the walls. I side-eyed these pictures.

Reco found me and began obviously flirting again, trying to win me over with that huge smile and his smooth words.

I shot him a what-are-you-doing? look. "Is that your wife?" I asked him, eying the pictures on the walls.

He burst out laughing. "What? No! That's my mom!"

I've got to admit, that softened me up a little. Any man who kept pictures of his mom all over his own house couldn't be all bad.

As the evening wore on, Reco asked me to "step into his office" to talk. I rolled my eyes and followed him with my friends nudging me eagerly. As he began to talk and talk and ask question after question, he then had the nerve to prop his feet up on his desk. I stopped him mid sentence to remind him that he wasn't talking to a "business prospect" and he could drop the fast talk.

He leaned back in his chair, lowered his feet, and just looked at me.

"How often do you give out your phone number?"

"I don't really. Hell, I didn't even give you my number."

"Good. Well, you don't have to worry about giving your number out to anyone else because you're going to be my wife."

I stared. And burst out laughing. "Boy, please. Who *says* that to someone you just met?"

"I do." He grinned with a sort of mischief, but also a sort of certainty. "I'm serious."

The conversation ended there, and eventually we all went home.

About a month went by and I didn't talk to Reco again. I was taking acting classes and while leaving class one day, a Jaguar car passed by. I called my friend to tell her about the slick car, and she reminded me that Reco had a "Jag" and that I should call him.

Well hell, I thought, *why not?* He hadn't been pestering me for dates like I'd been afraid he might.

My heart pounded a little as I pulled up Reco's number and hovered my finger over the "call" button. What would happen if I encouraged his pursuit of me? Was he already mad that I hadn't called or fallen all over him like so many women seemed eager to do?

Beep. I pressed the "call" button.

Ring ring. Ring ring.

"Hello?" My heart almost stopped when his deep voice came over the line.

There was staticky background noise behind him. He was at the airport, he explained. He was flying back to Atlanta and then he had to pick up his son, because it was his turn to have custody.

My stomach did a little backflip. I thought of my dad, how much I loved spending time with him when he could. I also thought of the horror stories I'd heard from women dating men who had "baby mommas," jealous exes who would do everything in their power to make the new girlfriend's life hell. I thought of the way my stepdad acted toward my dad, imagined being the stepmom. "You should come by when I get home," Reco proposed, interrupting my nightmare fantasies.

Reco still wanted to see me, even though it'd been a while since I last spoke to him.

"I'll think about it," I admitted, letting him hear the mix of pleasure and hesitation in my voice.

I called my friend back and she convinced me I should go over to see him because he could be my *Prince Charming*. I was not optimistic based on my experiences with men so far, but something made me go out there anyway.

To my surprise, I found myself *enjoying* Reco's company and conversation. I think he figured out the "I'm a big businessman" act wasn't working on me, so he dropped it. He turned out to be genuinely funny and charming, not in a "let me charm the pants off you," way but in an endearing, almost self-effacing kind of way.

And he *liked* me. I couldn't figure out why he liked me, with all the other girls at the party. Most of whom seemed prepared to fall all over him. In hindsight, maybe that was *why* he liked me: I wasn't too interested in his business or his money or his fancy car.

I am into cars. I can tell you a *lot* about cars and makes and models. I even dated a guy in high school and his family was known as "The Mustang" Family. They would rebuild and fix up mustangs and I'd go to car shows and races with them. I'd even eventually race myself. But I'd seen wealth used to manipulate people too many times for that alone to make me want to spend time with him.

We talked about Reco's car and why Jaguars weren't really very good anymore. Ford had bought their brand, so now they were running the same parts under the hood as any old American working car instead of the British luxury cars they had once been.

We threw playful little jabs at each other, laughing late into the night. He didn't even try to make a move on me, which made me question everything I had assumed about him: I'd assumed he would be a womanizer, but he seemed interested in me as a person. He really did seem interested in *only* me. And not in sex on the first date.

When I was with Reco, I felt seen and appreciated for who I was. Not for who the world expected me to be.

As I learned more about Reco, my feelings toward him shifted in complicated ways. For one thing, he had a son by another woman, and that terrified me. I had seen too many families become convoluted by that dynamic. Either because the man had a problem with commitment or as I stated before the "baby mama."

But Reco seemed different from the others. He told me about his son up-front, and proudly. In fact, he was often unavailable to talk because he was picking his son up or they were hanging out.

Reco had his anxieties about me as well. Though he seemed to have picked me out of the crowd from the moment he set eyes on me, I didn't exactly make myself easily available.

"Are you married?" he asked, half-joking and half-exasperated, on the phone one night. "You *only* talk to me when you're driving home from work."

"No!" I exclaimed, shocked. Of all the accusations I'd been expecting, that wasn't one of them. "I just have a lot going on! I work full-time, and I take acting classes, and I live with my parents!"

A pause. "And that's one of the things I love about you," he said.

Spending time with Reco was easy. Somehow I was comfortable with him. His discussions of the future set off some alarm bells, but somehow there never seemed to be any real fire behind those alarms.

Reco *admired* me. And he never pressured me into anything. He just knew what he wanted, and he was willing to go get it.

"When I propose to you," he teased me one day, "you're gonna cry."

"I will not," I scoffed. "I'll laugh in your face."

"No," he predicted, "you're gonna cry."

In the days that followed, I mulled over Reco's situation. He was working hard to be a good dad to his son, Reco Jr., and to all appearances was doing a really good job of it. I respected the hell out of that. It reminded me of my brother and father.

I watched and appreciated how hard my brother worked to be a good dad to his kids because he wasn't always dealt an easy hand, but through it all, my brother's dedication to being a good dad never wavered. I loved my own dad so much and appreciated having him in my life, even though he lived in California and I lived in Georgia.

But if I were to get involved with Reco in a serious way, I would be becoming the new girlfriend. *Maybe* even the stepmom. I didn't have the best experiences with the jealousy and competition that came with relationships like that. I'd seen too many children get attached to a parade of new adults, only to have each one disappear upon breaking up with their mom or dad.

If I was going to spend time with Reco, if I was even going to *entertain* the idea of dating him, I'd need to take it real slow. I'd need to find out what it meant to be "the new girlfriend."

I made one thing clear to Reco: meeting Reco Jr. was not an option until I *knew* this was going to be a serious relationship, one that felt like it would last. I wouldn't risk him getting attached to me or me attached to him until I was quite sure I was here to stay.

***

When I met Reco, my decision to drop out of college with one semester left was still fresh. There was so much stress of attending the school without my old friends. With cash flow that was inadequate. My mom had just had a surgery that turned out to be more serious than I had expected and she was hurt that I wasn't there for her. Again, I moved back in with my mom and my stepdad, and tensions immediately began running high.

My stepdad made me feel that I was undervaluing him over the network marketing business that Reco was involved with. I tried not to think about Reco. I tried not to see him. Some local women had already started referring to me as a "gold digger" because they found out I'd been to his house, and the last thing I wanted was to get into another relationship of debt and obligation with a man who felt like he owned me because he paid my bills.

I was certain that was what Reco planned, and what would happen if I gave in to his overtures.

For a while, I was reasonably happy with my post-college life. Having a full-time job and bringing in a full-time income while living with my mom and stepdad, I had more disposable income than I'd had in years. At work I had responsibilities, and that made me feel like I was actually *doing* something rather than studying theory so that I could have responsibility someday in the future. I could almost begin to feel like a successful professional, even though I knew my student loan payments for the degree I hadn't finished would start up soon.

All of it had me on edge. It had all become too much. But all of this did help me in one area. If there was one thing I knew, it was that I needed to be able to provide for myself if I wanted to be truly free to make the relationship choices that were best for me

Opening ourselves up to something different and letting down our walls can be an intimidating, but ultimately rewarding journey. You want to protect yourself from further hurt, and staying in your comfort zone gives you a sense that you can control something. Your comfort zone is basically a defense mechanism. In this chapter, what made the difference was me allowing myself to let my walls down and also trust myself, my feelings, and my decisions.

Letting down your walls is about vulnerability, courage, and learning to trust. I'm curious to hear your thoughts and experiences on this path. Let's dig a little deeper into this topic.

1. What are the biggest fears or anxieties you face when it comes to vulnerability? How do you manage them?

2. Do you think letting down your walls will change how you connect with others? If so, how?

3. Is there something in particular that feels difficult for you when it comes to being vulnerable and letting your walls down? What makes it challenging to let go of?

4. This journey of letting your walls down is often about learning to accept and embrace your vulnerabilities. What are you discovering about yourself and your needs through this process of trusting yourself more and letting others in?

5. What are some of the positive outcomes you've experienced from opening up? How has it changed your relationships or your outlook on life?

Remember: vulnerability is not a weakness, but a strength. I've learned through therapy that it takes courage to open up and be authentic.

Through the journey of letting your walls down and allowing yourself to be vulnerable, you have to have self-compassion. Be kind to yourself, and take moments to acknowledge that opening up is a process. There will be setbacks and moments of self-doubt, so celebrate every step forward that you take.

If you feel safe with your support system, I invite you to share your answers to the above questions and your own experiences with letting down your walls with your support system and lean on them. If you don't have a support system to lean on, I suggest sharing these answers with a therapist.

Chapter Nine

Eyes and Ears Wide Open

As the months passed, Reco slowly began to convince me that more was possible for me. And I don't just mean in the romantic realm.

As I spent more time with Reco, I began to learn more about his business team. They were his colleagues who he worked with day in and day out, so of course he talked about them.

A lot of people on Reco's teams didn't have degrees, and a lot of the highly competent, highly successful people around him had never gone to college. He and his team were of the opinion that results were ultimately what mattered, and that while education was important, formal education shouldn't be a barrier to accruing wealth.

And his team did bring in *stupid* amounts of money. More than I'd been led to believe was possible without a degree in business or medicine or something.

I wasn't part of "Reco's team" just yet. But just being around him, one picked up certain habits and certain expectations. People who were seen with Reco were expected to be highly professional. That meant moving with intention, kindness, and grace, and taking responsibility for one's actions.

I was starting to figure out that Reco's people were successful because they took this kind of radical responsibility for their lives. When something went wrong, they didn't look for somebody else to blame, and they didn't assume it meant they could never change. Instead they looked for what *they* could fix about the situation, and they fixed it. And in that way they slowly wrestled control of their lives from an environment where so many things were beyond our control.

I had to admit, I kind of liked it. The way they took responsibility for their own feelings was *such* a refreshing change.

Over the months that I dated Reco, he inevitably talked to me sometimes about how he felt his business model could improve my life. He knew I was frustrated with the obstacles that had prevented me from graduating from college, and he knew I was anxious about my financial future having student loans and no degree.

I'd made it clear in no uncertain terms that I would not let him pay for anything *for* me: I never wanted to feel indebted to someone again the way I had felt indebted to my stepdad over that apartment situation.

Besides, I hated the idea that Reco might think I liked him *because* of his money, when that was actually the biggest obstacle to me liking him. It was his money and his business success that had made me suspicious of him initially, even though he treated me right. And I couldn't stand the thought that he might suspect even for a second that I liked his money, not him.

So, I wouldn't let Reco buy me anything. Not even clothes. But I would, grudgingly, take his business advice. I didn't mind the idea of being able to make money for myself at all.

I was skeptical of Reco's claims that I could make money in his industry at first. He was in network marketing, like my stepdad, and my stepdad's attempt to get me into his network marketing business had ended with failure, blame, and recrimination.

But I was starting to figure out that my stepdad hadn't fully explained what was expected of me when he signed me up for his network marketing business. What I did get from him was a brief conversation about how the business model worked and its benefits. I needed more one-on-one training and details on what I needed to do exactly."

Well, now I wasn't a college student already trying to juggle studying full-time with a demanding job that provided me with a steady paycheck. Now I had time to think and do research.

I looked at the numbers Reco gave me for how people made money in his business, and how many people were making money. This didn't seem to be a pyramid scheme situation with a few multimillionaires at the top and a lot of people getting taken advantage of at the bottom. His company didn't seem to be pressuring people to spend huge amounts of money on things that wouldn't pay them back. They made the bar for entry very accessible, and the products and services they sold actually seemed to help their customers build up their own financial futures and save money.

I would research the company Reco worked with, wanting to get independent sources on their methods and reputation. But I always stopped if I was reading an article and I saw Reco's name.

I didn't *want* to know how much money he made. I never wanted money to be a determiner of what I could or could not do in a relationship again.

But everything I found looked encouraging. Reco and his team seemed to be wealthy, not because they were scammers using high-pressure sales tactics, but because they were scrupulous and community-oriented enough to have built a long-term reputation as being good people to do business with.

They had a method for selling, for planning ahead to ensure profit. And the more I learned about their products and services, the more I believed and understood that they were actually helping people.

I was beginning to believe that network marketing with *this* company could be for me, too.

There was just one problem. Over the months I dated Reco and listened to him talk about his business, I took a lot of notes. I filled a notebook with notes about this industry, how the cash flow worked, how sales strategies worked, how the product benefited customers and communities.

My stepdad found it and went through it, writing his own in the margins.

I was *devastated*.

To me, this was the last straw. It wasn't just about the notebook: this was a fundamental sign of disrespect for my things, my judgment, my ambitions, for my very *thoughts*. My stepdad was clearly angry that I was interested in network marketing with Reco when I had refused to work in network marketing under him.

I couldn't live with him anymore. I was slowly becoming aware that, no matter how hard I tried to be strong or disciplined, that kind of treatment was destroying me. That close relationship we once had in the beginning had ultimately deteriorated, and honestly speaking, through my anger I was sad this happened to our relationship.

Eventually I moved out to live with Monta.

I felt guilty about imposing on my brother, and I felt like a failure not being able to afford a place on my own. I would not, would *not* let Reco help me out of this. Reco knew the worst thing he could do for our relationship would be to try to swoop in and rescue me instead of letting me rescue myself.

This is where you found me, on the eve of my second suicide attempt. Still feeling like a failure as a student, a daughter, a professional, because after all the support I had been given I was still living in my brother's spare room. I was so aware that the friends I had gone to high school and college with, the ones I had always felt a little bit inferior to even when I was a high achiever on paper, were off with adult careers and families of their own already.

You know about the pills I took, and how I went out and sat in my car and waited to die. So we'll skip over that part.

But you *also* know that I didn't die. And I came away from it thinking that maybe, just maybe, two failed suicide attempts meant that I *did* have a God-given purpose after all.

I walked away from that car determined to succeed. God had dropped Reco McCambry right in front of me, and Reco thought I could learn everything I needed to to succeed in business. God had put women in my path who said I helped them, that I saw them and cared about them when no one else did. This was honestly more fulfilling to me, though I could not see any way to turn it into the sort of paying career that people defined themselves by.

Between these two things, maybe, I could still carve out a life worth living.

I joined Reco's team of professionals.

The first time he invited me to a conference, I dropped an entire paycheck on a couple of outfits off the sales rack to wear, gambling that if I switched up my combination of wardrobe items no one would notice that I only had two outfits across a three-day seminar. Life happened and I wasn't able to go.

As I began to come around more, attending the meetings, building my own business, I got noticed. Some of the women in Reco's circles who thought of themselves as potential romantic partners for him *especially* noticed our relationship.

One woman in particular was a part of Reco's leadership team. Unfortunately, it was also obvious to me from a million miles away that she had a crush on him, and for this reason she did *not* like me at all. This was the first real test of my own ability to handle myself like a professional.

After a number of team meetings where her disdain for me was obvious, I overheard her at a group function telling someone that she didn't understand why Reco would possibly want to be with me, romantically or professionally.

"She looks like a librarian," this woman was complaining. "She drives this old car. She's obviously only here for his money. And if he thinks she's gonna be able to perform up to the same level as the rest of us..."

Hearing her, I froze. This was nothing new to me, or exactly shocking. Women had been calling me a "gold digger" ever since it got out that Reco was interested in me. What did shock me was to hear such blatant criticisms stemming from such obvious insecurity coming from a member of Reco's *professional* team. He demanded a high standard of behavior from his people, and here was this woman openly trash-talking my looks and my less than wealthy background to our colleagues.

I had to think for a long minute about how to handle this. In college, this would have been a "I'm going to throw down with you right here in front of everyone" situation. The honor culture of college girls would have demanded an immediate rebuttal. But the professional world had different standards.

I waited until she was alone, and then I approached her with a smile on my face.

By the look on *her* face, I could see she wasn't happy to see me. I don't know if she figured out I'd heard what she was saying.

"Listen," I said to her sweetly, "I heard all that you have been saying. I am *not* a gold-digger. I am not someone you want to mess with. I have nothing against you, but if you continue trying to cause problems for me, I will. I am sure you don't want to see the other side of the "librarian". So I suggest you keep your negative opinions about me to yourself, if you don't want any trouble."

Anybody watching the conversation would have thought it was a friendly one, from my smile and my casual demeanor.

I walked away before she could respond, not trusting my own potential reactions if she said something stupid.

Almost as soon as I walked away, I was terrified. Old instincts came back. I was used to being on the wrong side of the power differential. This woman, after all, had more professional skills than me and was an essential part of Reco's business team. What if she decided to complain directly to Reco about what I'd said to her? Surely I couldn't win in a conflict between his crush on me and the business that was his life. I could lose Reco, and my opportunity to learn to excel in business, in one fell swoop. I should have just stayed quiet...

My fears proved to be unfounded. She *did* eventually stop trash talking me to our colleagues. We didn't interact with each other, other than a few looks shared at conferences or meetings.

Reco did ask me about the conversation I had with her. I was afraid he'd be upset that I had, in my own mind, caused drama within his leadership team. To my great surprise, he burst out laughing.

"*You* did that?" he said, like I was the least likely person in the world to pull a power move. "You crazy!" But the undertone in his voice said *'Good job!'*

Slowly, I began to realize that Reco genuinely did value me. He liked me for *who I was*, not for any fancy outfits or cars or professional skills I did or didn't have. Just like I liked him for *who he was*, and not for the wealth he *did* have.

For the first time, I began to really feel like enough. Not because I'd won enough accolades or awards, but because people actually *liked* me, even when I couldn't earn them money or when I had feelings that might be inconvenient for them.

I'd had a taste of this with my college friends, but with Reco it was different. Even with Tori and DeAndrea and Denise, I'd worried (baselessly) that I could lose their friendship if I said the wrong thing. With Reco, it was precisely the conflicts with his team that showed me that I *wouldn't* lose his love the second I became inconvenient.

I wonder sometimes what Reco saw in me that day at the barbecue. Could he tell, already, that I was someone who wouldn't harm others if I could possibly avoid it? That I genuinely wanted everyone to feel good about themselves? Could he somehow tell that I'd be cautious in my decisions and wouldn't take advantage of his love?

I can't know, but I do know one thing. I felt like I was finally being seen.

***

Months passed. Reco and I grew together, both in business and our personal lives. Either of us will be among the first to warn of the dangers of mixing business with pleasure. Money troubles can tear friends and family apart, and friendships can destroy businesses if one person isn't performing, and the other doesn't have the heart to fire them.

We managed to keep things separate. I was always going to be Reco's woman, even if I turned out to be terrible at network marketing. And if I did turn out to be terrible at it, I was prepared to remove myself from Reco's professional team in a heartbeat.

I started working as a visual acuity technician in an optometrist's office. This job paid decently, and it was very fulfilling: even though I didn't have a degree, I was able to perform tests that helped diagnose health problems and correct people's vision. Customers often walked out of our office looking and feeling like a million bucks, and I was able to be a supportive presence for them during the process.

The visual acuity technician job and being in network marketing paid me enough to live a decent life compared to how I'd been scraping by on a part-time minimum wage job in college.

It turned out I was actually pretty good at business things. I'd always been a critical thinker and something of an overachiever. I'd taken responsibility for my actions: maybe pathologically so, with the amount of blame I laid at my own feet for other people's actions and what I perceived as my own failures to excel.

It turns out, taking responsibility is the stuff that corporate executives are made of. Sometimes it doesn't even matter if you caused a problem: if you are the one who takes responsibility for fixing it, customers love that, and a boss who has any business sense at all will recognize you for it.

We didn't exactly do hierarchical job titles in Reco's organization at the time, network marketing being a business model where each person gets personal credit for their own sales and business decisions rather than following orders from a boss. But suffice to say, I more than pulled my weight. I was as surprised as anybody else, never having thought of myself as a businessperson.

Reco was thrilled. His intention in bringing me in the business had been to help me out. Now that I understood what his company did and how to do it, I was in a position where I could fully financially support myself and have freedom to make my own life choices.

One of those choices, of course, was Reco.

The better I got to know the guy, the more he grew on me. I'd come into our relationship with an aversion to businessmen and a profound suspicion of anyone who lived a flashy lifestyle. I'd been accused of being a gold digger just for taking an interest in him, which I knew would happen, and had been rather unkindly criticized by people around him who felt I wasn't good enough for him.

But.

I couldn't get his smile out of my head. His sense of humor. His realness and honesty when he got serious. Even while he was traveling around the country building and helping his team, he always seemed to have a mind for community service. He found time for *me*. His wealth and success never made him "untouchable". If anything, he seemed to be so wealthy and successful *because* he was considerate, because people knew they could trust him to do the right thing even when they weren't looking.

He continued to treat me well as our relationship went on, showing a level of respect for me as an individual that I honestly had assumed was impossible from someone who clearly didn't *need* me to fix some sort of problem in his life. I felt safe with him.

One date night, Reco and I were finishing dinner when he spotted a horse-drawn carriage pulling up to the curb. It was one of those elegant, novelty experiences. The carriage was trimmed in bright lights, with a driver dressed in sharp vintage finery and a comfy pair of seats facing each other in the carriage behind him.

"Hey, let's do that," Reco suggested, seeming taken with the old school charm of the thing. I had no idea yet that he had planned the whole thing, had hired the driver to be there at that place and time.

I happily agreed and he helped me up into the carriage. The driver started the impressive white draft horse on its way with a cheerful yell.

I looked out of the carriage at the sights of downtown Atlanta, marveling at the lights and the people walking by. We laughed and talked as the city rolled by. I must have slapped his leg a dozen times as we cracked up at our own jokes, and somehow I didn't feel the mysteriously angular lump in his pocket once.

As we approached a red light, I could hear gasps and '*awww's*' from the people walking by. I hadn't even noticed Reco glancing at me, perhaps a little bit nervously, and fishing around inside his pants pocket.

I was shocked to turn and see Reco down on one knee with an open ring box in his hand.

I think I screamed. I know I cried. When he told me two years earlier that I'd be his wife someday, I'd thought he was crazy. But now I wanted to be just that, his wife.

"Yes! Of course! Yes!"

That's the kind of resounding "yes" that I'd been missing.

I was going to be the next Mrs. Reco McCambry.

Now we just had a wedding to plan.

***

In this chapter, I saw the good things that can happen when you step outside your comfort zone. So we're going to focus on questions about moving out of your comfort zone.

We were not born to try to fit into a box and stay the same. We weren't designed for stagnation. We were created to evolve and grow.

These questions are about nurturing what's within you. They're about breaking free from the limiting boxes we might have built around ourselves, and embracing the growth that comes with stepping outside the comfort zone.

1. What makes you nervous or anxious? Identify areas where you shy away or feel apprehensive. These could be activities, skills, fears, or interactions.

2. What are your current strengths and weaknesses? When we take time to recognize our strengths, this can motivate us to keep moving towards certain activities and to give ourselves a pat on the back. When we understand our weaknesses, we can identify areas for growth.

3. What limiting beliefs do I have that are holding me back? Do any internal voices tell me "I can't," "I'm not good enough," "I'm too old to learn," or "I'm afraid of failure?" Challenge those messages by finding evidence showing that these beliefs are the opposite of true.

4. What is one thing that you have always wanted to do but haven't dared to try? Why haven't you tried it yet? Start small and try it out. Celebrate your progress on the journey to go do it!

5. What specific steps can you take this week to celebrate your strengths and incorporate them more fully into your life? Remember, it doesn't have to cost anything to do this. You don't have to go on a shopping spree. If you have been working hard and sleeping less, your celebration can be sleeping in late on your next day off.

6. What resources or learning experiences could help you develop your areas of weakness? What are some small, achievable steps you can take to improve? When you accomplish them, find ways to celebrate your progress and small wins.

7. Sometimes stepping out means letting go. What outdated perspectives or habits can you let go of to make room for the new ones?

Stepping out of our comfort zone is hard. I know it firsthand. There will be stumbles, moments of doubt, and days when the path ahead seems blurry.

But that's the beauty of the journey, isn't it? It's not about arriving at a *perfect* destination. It's about the courage it takes to keep moving, to learn from each stumble, and to find joy in the unexpected twists.

Chapter Ten

Something Old, Something New, Something Borrowed... Something's A Clue

I debated, when writing this book, whether to include the wedding planning at all. After all, the important bit can be summed up in one sentence: we were married. The wedding itself was not the site of any major drama or life-changing decision. Except, in a way it was.

Everybody who has planned a wedding knows that they can be the most fun you'll ever have, or your worst nightmare, and often they are both. Every detail of a wedding is considered to have some sort of significant symbolism about your life to come, as a married couple.

As a result, people fight like cats and dogs over the choices that are made while planning a wedding. Whose wishes are respected in a wedding is considered a sign of who has the power in a relationship. People who are insecure, or controlling, or power-hungry will take any opportunity to get offended at choices they perceive as disrespectful to themselves, and when you've got a big family involved there's bound to be at least a couple of those people.

For this reason, the wedding story is worth telling. It illustrates several power dynamics, and how I grew as I made decisions about how to handle those.

Reco and I originally wanted a destination wedding. But some of Reco's family had a crippling fear of flying, so we decided it was reasonable to have the wedding locally. A lot of our friends and family would have struggled to afford the cost if there had been airline tickets and resort hotel rooms involved anyway. Instead we chose a local golf course. Reco *loved* golf, and this course had several luxurious houses bordering the property.

Next was deciding who was and wasn't going to be in the wedding. Oh, what a headache this was.

I did not realize then that this was a classic people-pleasing mentality: that people who are insecure about their worthiness, about your love of them, will often spiral into anxiety and a sense of unworthiness if they aren't given the awards and honors they think are markers of a job well-done.

This might have had something to do with how hard I worked to get honors and awards early in my life, how I would beat myself up if I received grades lower than a B+, and with the depths of despair I spiraled into when I felt I wasn't measuring up by earning money or getting a degree. We've all felt "not good enough" at some point when we weren't given the highest accolades available.

Fortunately, Reco was showing me another way of thinking.

It was the question of alcohol that made me snap. I didn't want any alcohol at all at my wedding. I remembered how alcohol had killed my uncle J.P., not to mention the unruly behavior it could sometimes inspire in others. I knew that alcoholism ran in my family. With the large number of family and friends we were inviting, and the not-always-easeful relationships, I had literal nightmares about people getting drunk and getting into fights, or throwing up on the dance floor, at my wedding.

Unsurprisingly, some of our family members were shocked by the announcement that there would be no alcohol. An unfortunate number of adults to this day consider it impossible to really have fun or relax without alcohol, so from their point of view not having it defeated the entire purpose of a wedding reception. The objections were so bad that I began to worry: even if we didn't *provide* alcohol, would someone sneak it in and then get sloppy drunk in the middle of our special day?

I stressed about this so much that Reco sat me down for a serious talk about it.

"Look," he said, leaning toward me across the table, "you do what *you* want. If you say there's no alcohol, then there's no alcohol. If people bring alcohol in with them, they will be asked to leave. This is *our* wedding. No one is going to disrespect either of us and get to stick around."

I realized, suddenly, that the power *was* in my hands. This was a shocking realization as it moved through my body. Always, before, if I'd been responsible, I felt I was handling it on behalf of other people and I had to make my decisions based on what would benefit *them* the most. And that was the mindset I'd been applying to my own wedding, trying to figure out how to plan it so everyone *else* would be as comfortable as possible.

Opportunities to exercise that power continued to arise. One of my bridesmaids was married to a man who had recently decided to start taking the Bible extremely literally. As a result, he saw it as his place to decide whether or not his wife should be in my wedding—and agreed only on the condition that she would wear a long-sleeved, high-collared shirt *under* her bridesmaids dress "so that her collarbone would not be exposed."

I remember blinking, a little bit nonplussed, as he said this. *Now* what was I supposed to do? I hated the thought of one of my bridesmaids appearing in my wedding photographs with a full-on turtleneck *under* her dress. But if I said "no," would I lose my bridesmaid?

This is our *day.* I heard Reco's voice in my head. If my girlfriend herself had been asking about modesty concerns, it would have been different. But this was her husband asking, and I couldn't even tell how she felt about it at that moment.

"I'm afraid that won't be possible," I said, as coolly as I could. "I would love for your wife to be one of my bridesmaids. But I'm going to need all of my bridesmaids to meet the same wardrobe requirements."

I sighed inwardly. She had always been something of a fashionista; I should have known she wasn't any more excited about being immortalized in my wedding photos wearing a turtleneck under her dress than I was.

In the end, she was one of my bridesmaids, and her collarbone was uncovered.

On the other side, Reco challenged me pleasantly.

He wanted me to enter the wedding by dismounting from a horse-drawn carriage. I initially couldn't stand this idea. I couldn't stand it because I was still afraid of the criticism I'd take, of the offense I might give, if people thought I was acting "better than them."

I was worried about that on my own wedding day!

And here I learned to feel the difference between a "no" from inside me and a "no" from outside.

Did I really hate the idea of stepping out of a horse-drawn carriage with my dad as my entrance? No. I actually kind of loved it. What I hated was the idea that, if I was the center of attention, people would find a way to criticize me.

I knew that whenever I lifted myself up, some people would accuse me of being vain or selfish or tempting fate. And part of me *believed* them, because I'd been taught at some level to second-guess myself. To not trust my own judgment.

That last one was what I really hated. I hated the fact that I couldn't stand the thought of lifting myself up in front of everybody. So I let Reco coax me into that carriage ride.

I was so nervous about all the eyes on me as I sat in the carriage beside my dad, that he had to remind me to wave to our guests.

I wasn't expecting the carriage to do a full circle around the venue, promenading around with us on display, before circling back around to let us out. By the end of that carriage ride, my cheeks were burning.

But, as I stepped out of the carriage in my white dress to a chorus of "oohs" and "ahhs," I felt kind of good. Kind of like when I was homecoming queen.

This moment was much more meaningful: I'd been picked by my husband, not just by my classmates from school. It was the man beside me who really meant everything on this day. But there was that sensation again, of grudgingly admitting that I was beautiful and I *deserved* the spotlight.

The ceremony was beautiful.

My dad came out to walk me down the aisle. It was as though we'd never been separated.

Our mothers had been given a color to wear, but not a style of dress. We wanted each of them to express themselves, and they did: Reco's mother a spitfire in a halterneck-topped dress, my mother in a V-neck dress with a subtle wave to the skirt. To open the ceremony, Reco and I presented both of our mothers with bouquets of flowers to honor them. We gave Reco Jr. a stylish necklace to wear as he, too, accepted me as part of his family.

Reco and I were married on October 27th, 2007. My mom cried: a vanishingly rare event.

If this were a romance novel, that would be the happily-ever-after. But this is real life, and there were challenges I had never imagined ahead of us.

***

Things in life tend to come full circle time and time again. I had gotten to a good space where I was "comfortable" saying "yes" and "no." Then, when I decided to plan the entire wedding myself, I was faced with having to make many decisions that included saying "yes" and "no" more than I wanted. I was being tempted to say "yes" and "no" to others over choosing what it was that I really wanted.

This can be like driving in dense fog. You know you have to keep going through it, but you are unsure what's in front of you due to the limited visibility. You don't know what's going to happen while you're going through it, you pray it doesn't get thicker, and you hope you don't encounter any other vehicle or random animals. You make the adjustments necessary for you to drive safely and see as much as you can. And when you make it through, you feel a huge sense of relief.

Going through that foggy feeling and choosing to do what is best for *you* allows you to feel more inspired and empowered to take control of your decisions.

Let's dig a little deeper.

I really want to help you understand your triggers and develop strategies to help navigate them when they arise. This would be a great time to work with the journal that goes along with this book, just for you to fill with your thoughts and findings.

1. Does saying "yes" often leave you feeling drained, resentful, or obligated?

2. Does saying "no" trigger guilt, anxiety, or fear of disapproval?

3. Does this happen with work, family, social circles, or a specific person?

4. Does the "no" arise from a genuine conflict with your values or desires, or is it driven by fear of disappointing others?

5. Does your "yes" or "no" stem from fear of disappointing others, disapproval, or losing connections?

Taking a moment to recognize these emotional cues can help you untangle your internal feelings from outside pressures. Write down the first ones that come to your mind. Do not second guess your thoughts.

1. What brings you joy and fulfillment?

2. What aligns with your values?

3. What drains your energy?

4. What matters most to you?

5. What principles do you want to live by?

This self-awareness helps to clarify your personal priorities and build a foundation for authentic choices.

Let's come up with what I had to do, which was called a "filter plan." This filter plan helps you prioritize genuine "yeses" and "nos." It helps you avoid saying "yes" just to please others at your own expense. It also helps you realize that saying "no" isn't about denying others, but about protecting your own well-being and respecting your limitations. Saying "no" empowers you to prioritize your own needs.

Before saying "yes" or "no" to anything, ask yourself: "Is this aligned with my values and goals?" "Does it bring me joy or fulfillment?" "Am I able to fully do what I am being asked?"

Here are some reminders that might be helpful:

- Saying "no" is a skill that can be learned and strengthened with practice. Start small, with saying "no" to minor requests, and gradually build your confidence. You can say "no" in a nice way.

- Sometimes, instead of simply saying "no," explain your reasons briefly and respectfully. This helps manage expectations and sets healthy boundaries without being hurtful or dismissive. This is called assertive communication.

- Focus on the positive outcomes of assertive communication. Saying "no" opens doors to saying "yes" to opportunities that truly resonate with you and align with your goals.

- Setting boundaries and saying "no" is not selfish, it's an act of self-care. By prioritizing your needs, you create space for genuine connection and avoid depleting your energy.

- Embrace the power of "yes" to your true desires and values. Saying "yes" to experiences that ignite your passion fuels personal growth and unlocks new possibilities. Celebrate these "yeses" as stepping stones on your journey to self-discovery.

- Seek support and encouragement from trusted friends, family, or a therapist. Having a supportive network can help you navigate challenges and celebrate your progress.

The journey to becoming a confident, self-directed decision maker is a continuous process. Be patient with yourself, learn from your mistakes, and celebrate every step you take towards claiming your voice and living a life true to yourself filled with authenticity, purpose, and fulfillment.

By digging deep into the pros and cons of "yes" and "no," you can unlock a powerful tool for self-discovery and personal growth. I hope these questions and insights help you on this journey, and empower you to navigate the "yeses" and "nos" with confidence, authenticity, and self-compassion.

Chapter Eleven

Planted, Not Buried

I n the months to come, I continued to grow as a business-woman. That was still something of a foreign word to me. I had always envisioned myself as an employee—someone who performed a fixed set of skills and was paid a steady check by an employer who ultimately called the shots. I had never seen myself directly selling anything or being in charge of cash flow.

It was oddly empowering to realize that I could *sell*, that I could create revenue all by myself without a retail location or a supervisor to tell me what to do. I found that I could really understand how money moved, that I could make savvy business decisions.

I'd been raised to believe that you go to school, you go to college, and ultimately you get a good job. I mean this what the majority of people were taught to do and believe. Now that I had my hands in the lifeblood of the economy, I was really beginning to feel that I could support myself and make my own choices off the beaten path.

When I first joined Reco's team, he was selling telecommunications plans and equipment. I began to realize that this was the *perfect* time to be in telecommunication sales: in the late 2000s, technology was just reaching a place where wireless Internet and cell phones were becoming affordable to the average person.

Believe it or not, I grew up in an era where phone calls and Internet access had to share a single phone line in most households, and that dial-up Internet was so painfully slow that it was the main reason why image and video content weren't popular in the early 2000s. Nobody had a good enough Internet connection to load such massive files as a high-resolution photograph, let alone a video clip, in a reasonable amount of time!

That was changing in 2007, and Reco and I were positioned to make huge profits as technology advanced and we were already established as a trustworthy team to buy from, and a trustworthy team to join.

One could call this "luck," being at the forefront of the booming industry of the moment. But I soon learned that it wasn't luck. It was strategy. Reco had learned that being in the business of sales meant that you could move to sell whatever product appeared to you to have the most promise. The skills of business, sales, and customer relationships were largely the same, no matter what you were selling.

Initially, Reco and I didn't run a joint operation. We were part of the same team and we worked together where it made sense, but we each made our own sales to our own customers.

I had always been insistent about keeping our finances separate, and I wasn't eager to take orders from anybody, *especially* if they were family. But after getting married, we combined forces, and before long he and I were the second- and third-highest performing sales people in the network marketing company we were partnered with.

One thing that set us apart was that Reco and his team had very high standards of morals and ethics. We were determined to provide the best value they could to their customers and colleagues alike and believed that taking the high road and going above and beyond was the way to cultivate long-lasting trust with customers. If anyone behaved badly or broke promises to customers, that was a serious problem for our whole organization: beyond just being unacceptable to our spirits, it was a threat to our reputation and our customer satisfaction.

The troubling part was, not everyone in the industry acted that way.

I'm not sure if there was a shift in culture as the 2000s drew to a close, or if I just noticed the differences more as I got to know the industry better. But gradually, I began to realize that too many people in the industry were taking what I call a "fast money" approach.

These folks wanted to make as much money as they could for themselves, as fast as they could, with minimal effort. Now in a way, making as much money as possible with minimal effort makes sense. That's just efficiency, and it's what makes any operation profitable. But the problem came from the "fast" part.

Reco and I knew that the most efficient way to make money with minimal effort was to be trustworthy operators. We had an abundance of repeat customers, a huge volume of referrals, and a large growing team who believed in us, the vision, and a prosperous future because we had worked hard and with integrity. But that's not what these fast money folks were doing.

They weren't looking at the long-term. They weren't looking at "how do I create lasting good relationships and operate ethically." They were looking at "how can I sell as much as possible *right now* with minimal effort even if it meant taking advantage of people?" This led to a lot of false promises and salespeople who would sometimes straight-up lie to customers and then disappear on them to try to make a quick buck. People would lie to colleagues, misleading them about their prospects in the industry and leaving them in bad situations.

This sort of behavior is a large part of the reason why network marketing has a sketchy reputation in some circles today.

To be honest, I am of the opinion that this is the sort of behavior that is ruining the whole U.S. economy. It's far from restricted to network marketing spaces, and many of the stupidest and most unethical business decisions of the past 20 years have been based on this shortsighted obsession with *only* next quarter's profits.

They weren't thinking about next year's profits, or even the next five years. They weren't thinking about what was going to happen when their lives were exposed and nobody trusted them or their whole industry anymore. All they cared about was the amount on their bank statements.

Reco and I couldn't stomach that. We didn't want to be associated with that kind of behavior, and we didn't want to sound like we were defending organizations where that behavior was common. We decided we had to get out, and Reco decided it was time to start his own. It was important to him, and to me by that point, that he have complete control over the quality of the product he was selling and over what kind of behavior was tolerated from his company's representatives.

But that's another story for another time.

This isn't a business book. This is a book about my personal growth after a lifetime of getting the message from the world that I was not good enough, that my feelings were not "correct," that I could not trust my own judgment.

Imagine what it felt like for a little girl who grew up hearing all that and feeling all of that, to find that she could bring in tens of thousands per month, not by doing as she was told, but by using her own judgment and making her own decisions.

I was not just being *told* that I was good enough: I was beginning to believe it.

Realizing just how much money I was bringing in was an odd kind of struggle. I was so used to barely scraping by that I still thought and acted like I was struggling. It was like cognitive dissonance, but instead of justifying something bad, I was unable to understand something good.

I remember the first time I bought a new car when I finally started making money. I'd been driving a car that was older than I was, and was grateful to have a reasonably reliable set of wheels that wasn't visibly falling apart. So when the time came to get a new car, I set my sights low. Too low, according to Reco.

"Now, you don't have to get a luxury car," he told me one day, after he caught me looking at used cars on the Internet. "But at least pick out what model and what color you want."

I looked up at him. "Any Toyota will do," I insisted. "As long as it's newer than that old Honda out there."

"No." He shook his head stubbornly. "You are successful. You get to have *preferences*. What *color* Toyota do you want? What color brings you joy?"

I thought about it. "Blue," I said finally. Both because the color blue is my favorite, and because I'd read somewhere it was the least likely color of car to be pulled over by police. My survival instincts were still very much driving my decisions.

Later, even that would change. At the time, Reco always had red cars, with shiny rims. Flashy, luxury cars, and a color that attracted cops. I finally drove his luxury car and it was a beautiful drive. Not like my Honda that would shake if you went over 65mph and don't you dare drive over 85mph.

While in California one summer, I saw a Lexus IS 300, and fell in love. That became my dream car when I was younger, but I never thought I'd get it, let alone deserve to drive it. So instead of getting that Lexus IS300, I got a Lexus GS350. It was two levels up from my previous dream car. It was red of course but I loved it. It was my first taste of luxury in a vehicle.

Now that things were changing in my life, spiritually, mentally, physically, and financially, I began to believe that maybe I had a *right* to be noticed, to attract attention, without fearing that I was doing something wrong.

What I'm trying to say here is, the road to becoming Chief Operating Officer made me a more complete woman. I'm not sure if that statement sounds ridiculous or cliche, but it's true.

Becoming successful in business taught me that I was competent beyond my wildest dreams. I didn't need to follow orders or rely on others to tell me what to do to become successful. I *did* need to develop my knowledge and my skills, and be coachable, but this wasn't some mystical achievement that was forever just beyond arms' reach. It was well within reach: it just took the discipline to take responsibility for the consequences of my actions.

Realizing that I was competent began to undo some of that childhood trauma. With all the evidence piling up before my eyes, I could no longer deny that I was *powerful*, not in the sense of having power over other people but in the sense of being able to make things happen on my own.

And as I realized that I was deserving and worthy of all things I wanted, that I was powerful, I began to understand that I didn't need to be afraid anymore. I did not need to *depend* on anybody's approval, so I didn't have to watch my every move, the way I dressed, the color of my car.

I could live for me, and the family I had chosen. The family who supported me and helped me step into my power and my worth, instead of holding me back.

Finally. Finally, I was free. I was *seeing* me the way God created me.

***

Setting expectations is key in life, from personal relationships to professional endeavors. Having expectations and standards provides clarity and direction, and prevents misunderstandings. Clear expectations eliminate guesswork and ambiguity. They provide a sense of accountability, motivating everyone to perform to the best of their abilities.

We are often led by social expectations set by others. But what expectations do you have set for yourself and your future? What will you and won't you accept in both your personal and professional lives? Expectations should evolve, just like you. But never lose sight of your core values and desires.

In one of my therapy sessions, I was told that my expectations should:

1. Provide directions that guide my decisions and actions towards my desired outcome.

2. Feed my motivation in achieving my goals, keeping me energized and focused, and propelling me in a positive direction when faced with challenges.

3. Enhance resilience because I know I will experience setbacks and they better equip me to handle the setbacks and bounce back stronger and wiser.

4. Shape my reality and expectations, because ultimately

they are what influence and shape how I perceive experiences and opportunities and interact with others.

5. Create accountability by setting standards for myself and holding myself accountable for my personal growth and self-mastery.

Okay, it's time to get your journal again. Let's begin creating your own expectations. Create expectations that don't limit but liberate you on your journey and fuel your potential.

These questions may look familiar from the beginning of the book. I invite you to answer them again here, to see if your answers are still the same:

1. What are your core values? Identifying your core values sets the foundation for your expectations. What are the principles that guide your life? What matters most to you?

2. What are your dreams, goals, and desires? Dream BIG and then figure out what is necessary to achieve it. What's the ideal career, relationship, or lifestyle you desire?

3. What do you need to do to meet those dreams, goals, and desires? Expectations aren't about reaching a predetermined finish line but about embracing the journey and the steps you take along the way. Identify milestones, celebrate small victories, and adapt your expectations as you learn and grow.

4. What is your outlook? Instead of dreading potential failures, frame your expectations around successes you want to achieve. Set expectations that stretch you beyond your comfort zone, but don't let them become chains that weigh you down. Expect progress, not perfection. Fuel your expectations with optimism, but don't ignore the realities of life and its challenges. A balanced approach encourages resilience and keeps you grounded.

5. What is your inner voice telling you? Ultimately, your expectations should resonate with your gut feeling. If something feels off, don't be afraid to adjust or even let go. Your intuition is a powerful guide.

Remember, your expectations must be created with intention and upheld with commitment.

May your expectations and standards become more than just wishes. May those around you respect and honor them just as you do.

Chapter Twelve

Closed Door, Opened Window

Being married gave me a sense of security. Reco and I immediately began talking about trying for a baby, but I was not optimistic. On top of my decade-old "tilted cervix" diagnosis, a more recent gynecologist had cautioned me that my uterine lining might be too thin after all the years I had spent on hormonal birth control pills. A thin lining can make it difficult for the body to handle the demands of supporting both an embryo and a growing fetus.

If you are reading this and you are on contraception, don't panic! It turns out that there are things you can do to offset this. But the point was, as 2007 drew to a close, I was not optimistic about having a baby of my own.

I was, however, thinking about other things. Other ambitions I had left behind.

In January 2008, I reached back out to Georgia Southern's admissions office about finishing my college degree. I knew I would make less as a teacher than I had been making in network marketing, but it wasn't about the money. It was about proving to myself that I could do it: I could finish college, and I could embark on the work of teaching and supporting the next generation.

It was honestly crazy to me to have options. Once, the question was, "How can I possibly afford to finish college?" Now the question was, "Am I willing to take the pay cut that comes with doing so?" "Will I have to move closer to Georgia Southern for classes?"

With my business under me, I could make choices freely, based on what I actually felt called to do. And the answer was, "Yes! I want to do this!"

On top of my newfound financial freedom, I got lucky. Georgia Southern announced that they would let me finish my degree in *only* one semester—I wouldn't have to re-take any of the classes I'd completed years ago.

But I was down to the wire. As it turned out, I had applied to go back to school at the last possible second. And that was particularly challenging because this final semester was the student teaching semester. That meant they didn't just have to find me a student desk to sit at: they had to find me a *teacher's* desk, a classroom somewhere in their network of schools that needed a student teacher with my qualifications and specialties.

This is how I ended up being placed at a school in central Georgia, a full *2 hour* commute *each way* from Atlanta.

I was torn about what to do when my assignment came in. I didn't want to drop out of school *again*: that would feel like establishing an unbreakable pattern, like something I couldn't go back from. But I couldn't exactly just conjure up a different school for me to work at to meet my graduation requirements.

On the other hand, I also couldn't drive four hours every week day to get between work and home.

What I *could* do, thanks to our business income, was rent an apartment close to the halfway point between my home with Reco and college. This would cut my morning and evening commute down to "just" two hours round trip, while making it possible for me to drive "just" one hour to see Reco and Reco Jr. on weekends.

I didn't like the idea of living separately less than a year after Reco and I had gotten married. As it turned out, he didn't like it either but was open to the idea. After weighing my options, I decided it was best to just make the drive each day. Hey, I like road trips, I had a reliable car. It was all in how you look at it, right?

I love the school I was assigned to for my student teaching position. I feel I had the best teacher to be assigned to and eventually would take over her class for a period of time as part of the requirement to graduate and earn my degree in Middle Grades Education. As the weeks wore on, I found myself perpetually exhausted. This obviously made sense to me at some level: I was dealing with a *lot*, and waking up extra early to make that 2-hour drive each morning and then the 2-hour drive home. But one of my colleagues had another idea.

"Damn, Shaneé," she asked, watching me blink blearily over my morning hot tea at my desk one day. "You pregnant or something?"

My eyes went wide. "I—what? No!" I touched my belly uncertainly. "At least...it doesn't seem likely."

She studied me with the wisdom that only street smart women have. "Nah," she announced, "you pregnant. It was the same way for me when I was."

I shook my head, putting the thought out of my mind. Fatigue in the face of demanding circumstances was nothing to get your hopes up over.

Except.

A few days later, I was driving home when I drove through a cloud of the most overpowering stench I had ever encountered. It was so bad I began to gag, and nearly vomited right there in the driver's seat of my shiny new Lexus. I looked around in disgust, wondering what the source of that horrible smell could be.

It was at that point I realized that what I was smelling was a nearby Burger King drive-through.

What did they do to their burger recipe? I wondered in horror. *It's never smelled like that before!*

I drove on, only to be assaulted by another wall of stink. My head began to pound as I inhaled some kind of rancid, acrid odor.

What the hell...? I looked around in confusion, and this time I saw a McDonald's sign. And realized that what I was smelling was French fries.

Oh. It's not the Burger King that changed. OH.

My mind ground to a screeching halt and my tires squealed as I turned into the next drug store parking lot at top speed. I bought a whole handful of pregnancy tests.

The only reason I didn't take the first one right there in the drug store bathroom was that I wanted to make sure I did it *right*. I'd heard of false positives and false negatives, and both possibilities terrified me. So I took the pregnancy tests back to my house, and hid them so Reco wouldn't find them and get his hopes up too soon.

When I woke up the next morning, I grabbed a pregnancy test from under my bathroom counter and practically ran into the toilet room. This was what the instructions said to do: use your first urine of the morning, after you've had eight hours of sleep for the pregnancy hormones to gather in your bladder.

I forgot to breathe as I watched to see which word would appear on the little blue stick.

One...two!

Pregnant!

I couldn't believe it. I didn't *dare* to believe it. I'd spent my life since the age of thirteen doubting whether I'd ever be able to have children. Even as I stared at the positive pregnancy test in my hands and reviewed my symptoms in my head, it was difficult to believe.

When I finally did believe it, I let out a whoop of joy.

Then I ran to the bedroom to show Reco.

***

If this were a made-up story, that would be the end. But this is real life, and real life is never perfect.

A few weeks after celebrating my ability to get pregnant against all odds, I woke up with horrible pains in my belly. I went to the bathroom, and was horrified to discover that I was bleeding.

Reco drove me to the emergency room, where it was confirmed: I was miscarrying my first child, just shy of my second trimester.

The emergency room staff treated the whole thing as horribly routine. You could tell that they saw this every day. No one had a sense of urgency while we waited to be assigned a room, and there was no real discussion of the emotional impact of a miscarriage on a would-be mother. The only warnings they did give me were about my *physical* care, about what I should and shouldn't do with my body as I recovered. The information that was given was a bare minimum.

I have never ceased to feel the pain of that loss. Not entirely. When I hear children laughing or pass a children's playground, I still feel pangs of grief. Who would that child have been if they had lived? How different would my experience have been, raising them alongside my other children? What potential was lost that night, while doctors and nurses treated me as an afterthought while I miscarried.

Yet in a strange way, it was that loss that led to me becoming the person I am now.

My miscarriage pushed me into a depression that required therapy. Reco and I began seeing a counselor who was ultimately able to encourage us to confront my abuser. That's another story for another time, but know that it happened: I got to tell him everything he had done to me with that abuse, and with the situation it created where I was blamed instead of him.

It was the pain of my miscarriage that led me to finally begin to speak publicly about my history. I spent years keeping quiet about it, feeling that no one would want to hear about my pain, or that I dared not draw attention to myself over tragedy. Finally, my therapist pushed me to post about my miscarriage on my budding social media page.

The response blew me away. Instead of being criticized or ignored, my story was shared widely. It turned out there were millions of women who had suffered the same kind of loss, who had suffered the same feelings in silence. They didn't see themselves represented in the media. They didn't hear anybody talking about the pain of miscarriage on TV. And they felt like I had for so long, that it just wasn't something that they could talk about. Maybe their grief wasn't even normal. Maybe it meant something was wrong with them.

Seeing the response to that post was what made me realize I had a responsibility to share my story. It wasn't just my miscarriage: so much else had happened to me, where I had suffered in silence for so long. I knew so well what it was to feel that your grief or pain is abnormal, to feel low despite having a life that many other people envy on the outside.

I knew then that I couldn't remain silent anymore. If seeing and caring about other women was my work, that started with seeing and caring about *myself* in those younger years. Not until I could look at and share what I had rejected in myself, what I had felt forbidden to talk about, could I help the rejected and forbidden parts of other women feel seen and validated.

***

In this final activity of the book, I want to share two things outside of my faith and support system that have helped me tremendously. These are affirmations and meditation.

Affirmations are declarations of faith or belief. They are positive statements that are repeated to ourselves that promote self-belief, motivation, well-being, and truth. They are typically "I am" or "I will" statements.

Meditation is the practice of taking moments to gather peace, focusing and training the mind to achieve a state of increased awareness, calm, and emotional stability. It helps to detach from distracting thoughts and emotions. There are many forms of meditation, but my favorite is called *Mantra Meditation*. This is when you repeat a specific word or phrase to quiet the mind, often with peaceful and relaxing music playing.

I included some affirmations at the end of Chapter 6, and I am including more below. But I encourage you to take a moment and write some of your own.

Say them in the morning and at night before bed. When the day is a challenging day, take a moment to say a prayer and then say some affirmations. Refocus your thoughts and mindset.

I am also including a guided meditation here. I suggest you record yourself reading the meditation and then play it for yourself when you need it. Find moments to meditate. I meditate before bed, after exercising, when your anxiety increases, and when you just need to have a moment of peace.

Chapter 12 Affirmations:

1. My mistakes are stepping stones to my success.

2. I am worthy of love, respect, and happiness.

3. I radiate positive energy and attract like-minded people.

4. I celebrate my victories, big and small.

5. I am grateful for the journey of personal growth, even the stumbles and setbacks.

6. I release negativity and embrace the joy of being alive.

7. I am learning to love and accept myself, flaws and all.

8. I forgive others and let go of resentment.

9. I embrace that difficulties are temporary, but my growth is permanent.

10. I release doubt and fear, knowing God's plan for me is greater than my understanding.

11. God's blessings flow freely into my life, and I welcome them with open arms.

12. I was made in God's image, and I am worthy of God's abundance in my life.

Now, create some affirmations of your own:

1.

2.

3.

4.

5.

Meditation

Find a comfortable position: You can sit cross-legged or some people say "criss cross applesauce" on the floor, on a chair with your feet flat on the floor, or even lie down if you prefer. Make sure your spine is straight and your body is relaxed.

Close your eyes or soften your gaze: Allow your focus to turn inward, away from any external distractions.

Begin with your breath: Breathe in. Now in your head, count to five slowly. Hold your breath and count to four slowly. Finally, blow out your breath and count to five slowly. Notice the gentle rise and fall of your chest. Feel the cool air as you inhale and the warmth as you exhale. Don't try to control your breath, simply observe its natural rhythm.

Focus on your body: Scan your body from head to toe, paying attention to any sensations you experience. Notice any areas of tension or tightness, and focus on relaxing those areas. Notice how when you breathe out those begin to relax more and more.

Imagine a peaceful place: Think of a place that brings you a sense of peace and tranquility. It could be a real place you've visited, a dream landscape, or even simply a serene state of mind. Immerse yourself in the details: the sights, sounds, smells, and textures. Feel the calmness of this place surrounding you.

Let go of thoughts and worries: As thoughts arise, acknowledge them without judgment and then gently let them go, like clouds drifting across the sky. Don't get caught up in their stories, simply return your attention to your breath and your peaceful place.

Repeat a calming mantra: Repeat a calming mantra or phrase silently to yourself. If you want to say it out loud, make sure it is just slightly over a whisper. Some examples include: "I am calm," "I am at peace," "I breathe in peace, I breathe out stress," or "Let go and let be."

Stay in this state of calmness for as long as you like: There is no right or wrong amount of time for this meditation. Simply enjoy the feeling of serenity and stillness. Mediations can last for 5 minutes or 15 minutes.

Gently come out of the meditation: When you feel ready, take a few deep breaths and slowly bring your awareness back to your surroundings. Open your eyes, if you closed them, and wiggle your fingers and toes. Carry the feeling of peace with you throughout your day.

***

I've been through a lot in this book, huh? Maybe so have you. Most of us start our adult lives with some kind of trauma in our past. Many of us start out feeling unworthy, or "not good enough."

The reasons for that are many. It can be the survival skills our families learned in the bad "good" old days or the injustices of the modern day. It can be people who actually meant harm, or people who wanted to help but didn't know how.

The important thing is, we are all here together. And we are all learning our own lessons all the time. For me, part of my calling is to teach mine—to teach what I have learned from experience, in the hope that it might save somebody some time. Or just help somebody feel seen in the darkness of a life where they're afraid to step into the light.

My message in this book is that it's okay to choose yourself. Many of us are taught that it's *not* okay to set boundaries or have needs. Many of us have been taught that we are worthy only when we are obeying or serving others.

And there's the trick of it. Because "serving others" *is* fulfilling. But "serving others" doesn't just mean doing whatever you're told. Sometimes what "others" need is to be told "no." Sometimes what the world needs is for *certain* people to be told "no," so that we can find our larger purpose.

I would not have been able to serve the way I'm serving now if I had done what I was told when I was younger. I would not have learned these skills, or come into my power, or seen the needs nobody was addressing if I had followed the path that was laid out for me. I wouldn't be able to share my story, or stand before you today, if I was too afraid of hurting someone's feelings to speak my truth.

In other words, I wouldn't be able to serve you now if I had not first chosen myself, chosen to do what *I* needed and what *I* thought was right.

Life is not a straight line. It is filled with valleys and victories. We're going to stumble, we're going to make some bad choices, and some of us will carry scars that run deep from pain and loss. The lie that we have been told and taught is that time heals all wounds. The truth is, time cannot heal all wounds nor can it erase them. The healing comes from changing how we view things, our mindset, our willingness to take the steps to dig deep and get to the root of it all.

Yes, the past whispers in our ears and reminds us of what happened, but it does not have to define us or our purpose. Our pain, though real and valid, does not have to dictate our promise. The people who may have wronged us or hurt us do not hold the key to our passion.

I have been through a lot, and I know without any doubt, there are many people who have gone through much, much more than

I have. I am sure they too have wanted to give up when times got so rough. My tough times have allowed me to appreciate the great times and to also give me moments to pat myself on the back for my resilience, growth, and perseverance.

I am proud of the woman I have become. I know I have more room to grow and evolve and look forward to doing just that. I know I will have moments of regression, doubt, and self-sabotage because I am human, I am a work in progress, and I have been through high highs and low lows. The important thing is to bounce back and have people in my life that will help catch me when I fall and encourage me to get back up. But it has to be ME and MY decision to do so.

Despite it all, I believe God has given us a pen to rewrite the story of our lives. He gave us a pen, not a pencil, so we won't focus or waste time trying to go back and erase the past, the lessons that come with it, or the setbacks, disappointments, or unmet goals. What we can do is turn the page and begin a new chapter. Leave the old chapters there because they hold lessons, scars that tell stories of strength and resilience while evolving.

If I could leave you with these as final thoughts. The setback may not be your fault, but the comeback is your responsibility. So unleash the power within to go after your God-given purpose. And, remember, God makes no mistakes.

That includes you.

About the Author

Shaneé McCambry is a proud mother of three, business owner, and women's empowerment advocate. She resides with her husband, Reco McCambry, her children Reco Jr., Raegan, and Rylee, and always acknowledges her one child up in Heaven. She currently serves as the Chief Operating Officer for Novae. She is a member of the International Association of Women, 100 Women In Finance, and Dell Women's Entrepreneur Network. She has been featured in Yahoo! Finance, Black Enterprise, VoyageATL, Who's Who In Black Atlanta, and more.

Shaneé is passionate about empowering and uplifting women and has been frequently invited to speak about women's empowerment, as well as hosting her own two day women's empowerment conference, Women That Win. Building others up is one of her greatest passions. She loves inspiring others to see their own greatness, strengths, potential, and growth. She is intentional about sharing her continual journey of working on herself, finding ways to love all of her perfect imperfections, her faith, and genuinely wanting to make sure that she is a light in the lives of those she comes into contact with.

Made in the USA
Columbia, SC
23 September 2024

42219017R00098